Workbook for Preventing Catastrophic School Violence

Also by the Author
The Truth About School Violence: Keeping Healthy Schools Safe
Catastrophic School Violence: A New Approach to Prevention

Workbook for Preventing Catastrophic School Violence

Jared M. Scherz

ROWMAN & LITTLEFIELD
Lanham • Boulder • New York • London

Published by Rowman & Littlefield
A wholly owned subsidiary of The Rowman & Littlefield Publishing Group, Inc.
4501 Forbes Boulevard, Suite 200, Lanham, Maryland 20706
www.rowman.com

16 Carlisle Street, London W1D 3BT, United Kingdom

Copyright © 2014 by Jared M. Scherz

All rights reserved. No part of this book may be reproduced in any form or by any electronic or mechanical means, including information storage and retrieval systems, without written permission from the publisher, except by a reviewer who may quote passages in a review.

British Library Cataloguing in Publication Information Available

Library of Congress Cataloging-in-Publication Data is available

ISBN 978-1-4758-1242-8 (pbk. : alk. paper)
ISBN 978-1-4758-1243-5 (electronic)

∞ ™ The paper used in this publication meets the minimum requirements of American National Standard for Information Sciences Permanence of Paper for Printed Library Materials, ANSI/NISO Z39.48-1992.

Printed in the United States of America

Contents

Preface: How to Use This Workbook — vii
Introduction — ix

Section I: Assessing Existing Prevention — 1
1. Armed Guards — 3
2. Surveillance and Intelligence — 7
3. Metal Detectors — 11
4. Zero-Tolerance Policies — 15
5. Peer Mediation — 19
6. Antibullying Campaigns — 21
7. Mental-Health Specialists — 25
8. Threat-Assessment Teams — 27
9. Restorative Justice — 29
10. Overview and Conclusions — 33

Section II: Building a Prevention Paradigm — 43
11. Theory and Violence Prevention — 45
12. Involving Parents — 49
13. Using Technology Safely — 65
14. Harnessing Social Media — 71
15. Early-Warning Violence Detection and Prevention — 79
16. Potential-for-Violence Inventory (PVI) — 83

Preface: How to Use This Workbook

This workbook is intended to serve as a pragmatic guide to evaluating your existing violence-prevention program and/or deciding upon a new approach. As you read through the pages of this book, pay attention to:

1. What resistance am I feeling toward this particular idea?
2. What are the barriers to implementing these ideas?
3. What do these barriers tell me about our school and school system?
4. What support will I need to embark on this transformational journey?
5. What might my school look like if I experiment with these ideas?

This workbook is intended to stimulate your thinking and expand your perspective. Attempts to operationalize complex concepts of the main book into more manageable objectives that are simpler to institute are made throughout.

After reading each chapter, consider the following exercises:

1. Create a polling system in your school that solicits dialogue on the varied topics (i.e., How would metal detectors likely impact the potential for violence in our school?). You can use the uframes from www.ufeud.com to set up these discussions on private websites for the school. While schools are often afraid to involve students and/or parents in questions of this magnitude, the opportunity to express and differ will begin the process of peaceful negotiation that will help to reduce violence potential in your school.
2. Bring the topics up during faculty meetings to begin meaningful discourse among the faculty. The effective school leader will become more adept at facilitating these types of meetings, which will help improve the decision-making and negotiating process for schools.
3. Weave questions about school safety into the curriculum. Encouraging kids to do research on important questions—such as the efficacy of deterrence methods like armed guards—can spark student awareness of violence prevention to a new level.
4. Consider how the school is addressing technology, both as a teaching tool and as an instrument for social change. If your school is not providing instruction on the safe use of social media and other technology, it's time to rethink the potential problems of ignoring this issue.

5. Check to see how much time is spent each day and week in proactive measures to improve school culture. If organizational health is not part of your vision/mission statement, consider how you might rework this guiding document upon completion of the book.

Introduction

On October 21, 2013, a middle-school student in Nevada shot and killed a teacher and wounded two other students before killing himself. In the CNN article describing the event is an embedded link to a seminar being conducted by Defensive Tactics Solutions, teaching teachers how to defend themselves and their students.[1]

The seminar begins with a fake gun being pointed at the head of one of the audience members, with the idea to take away the fear. The seminar goes on to tell the educators they have three choices in the threat of danger—to run, hide, or fight. For the purpose of this seminar, educators are taught how to treat the student like an enemy, where it's your life or theirs.

This is where we have evolved as a nation, putting valuable school dollars into turning our educators into tactical defenders whose job it is to save other students by eliminating the threat, even if that threat is a child. Whether or not this is a smart use of time and money is a judgment call. If it saves just one life, it's arguably worth it. But what if the money spent on this prevention strategy means less money that goes into another?

This is the case with many different strategies ranging from arming teaches to peer mediation, each offering a different philosophy-driven modality on keeping schools safe. Decisions around violence prevention may be an actual matter of life and death, so understanding the benefits or limitations of existing strategies or anticipated ones needs to be high on every school district's priority list. In addition to the tremendous financial investment, this is a decision that can ultimately protect a school from both long-term and immediate threats to teacher turnover, academic success, and of course school safety, so it needs to be made with tremendous care and forethought about the big picture.

In the proceeding chapters, a number of different options are described, along with their benefits and limitations, to help the decision makers of each school better navigate this increasingly important part of education. Keep in mind there is a difference between behaviors generated by learning and behaviors generated by deeper underlying feelings. For behaviors that are learned, such as theft, retaliation is a learned behavior requiring a different approach to reduce the potential this will turn violent. Retaliation may be learned as a justifiable response to being disrespected, and attention to deeper feelings may not prove as useful as a strong process for corrective action. For violence prevention that is mostly about behavioral modification, deterrents, reward, consequences, and skill building are going to be more effective because they provide parameters for remuneration.

For behaviors that are generated out of deep-seated emotions, these strategies will prove less effective, because the wounded child is acting violently from a sense of despair, without hope that his pain will dissipate. For those who are undergoing a more intense psychological deterioration, engaging in delusional violence, effective prevention efforts are born out of recognition rather than strategy. For those children seeking notoriety because they feel insignificant, it's unclear what prevention approach will help other than improving a school culture until the school is a place where everybody feels valued and has a mechanism to address this should they feel marginalized.

Systemic violence is aggression born out of practices, procedures, and organizational dynamics that adversely impact learning and will not be helped by any violence-prevention strategy. Difficult to determine and highly pejorative, this real threat to our public schools is addressed in the subsequent section on organizational health. What we want to be on the lookout for are implemented programs that promise to make schools safer but in fact add to an already unhealthy set of dynamics that in essence could do more harm than good.

As you read through the different strategies and approaches, keep in mind that violence is varied and that the individual motivators to act aggressively can vary widely, requiring schools to avoid complacency with any one solution.

NOTE

1. Kim Segal, "Teachers Train to Face School Shooter," *CNN Living*, September 30, 2013, http://www.cnn.com/2013/09/30/living/schools-teacher-shooter-defense-training/.

Section I

Assessing Existing Prevention

ONE
Armed Guards

With each real and perceived threat to our children's safety, the frantic call for greater security echoes through the virtual corridors of media and social media. Parents panic, amplified by news headlines that question why we can't keep our children safe. Lawmakers respond to the outcries of their constituents and the pressure from media by enacting new laws intended to have immediate results. At the forefront of the reflexive responses is the introduction of more stringent security measures.

About one-third of our nation's schools—23,200 in the 2009–2010 school year—already have armed guards. Since the 2012 massacre in Newtown, Connecticut, many more schools are considering joining the list, as well as reviewing their overall security protocols such as entry procedures and lockdown drills.

Among the considerations for greater security is the simple but complicated idea of stationing armed guards in schools. While some urban schools have an existing police presence, many are lacking any security personnel, raising the question of private-security personnel to establish a powerful presence in the building.

This may seem a simple idea for schools that can afford it. Armed guards present a visual deterrent for any who might consider bringing a weapon to school or acting violently. Armed guards may also act quickly to intervene when aggression occurs to prevent escalation. Armed guards may also serve as a refuge for those students who are bullied, allowing them to feel more confident in addressing the mistreatment before they take on a retaliatory posture.

Creating safer schools by introducing trained security officers has sparked intense debate across the country. Fueling the debate was the powerful voice of the National Rifle Association (NRA), who in the early part of 2013 expanded this idea in dramatic fashion. The NRA proposed training and arming teachers throughout the school system.

Former GOP congressman Asa Hutchinson, who headed the NRA-backed School Safety Shield, claimed the plan to train school personnel to carry firearms in schools was a common-sense way to prevent shootings like the December massacre in Newtown. With a nation still raw and exposed from this horrendous event, the suggestion resonated with many.

The NRA-backed National School Shield Program to train and arm school staff to prevent mass casualty shootings in schools served to instantly intensify the existing debate about armed guards. NRA Executive Vice President Wayne LaPierre stated, "The only thing that stops a bad guy with a gun is a good guy with a gun." He went on to ask "Why is the idea of a gun good when it's used to protect our president or our country or our police but bad when it's used to protect our children in their schools?"[1]

Whether it's arming school teachers or our citizens, we are dealing with a philosophical belief as much as a strategic intervention. About as polarized as any debate in American society, it tends to be stratified according to geography. Those in the southern and midwestern states are greater advocates, while the remaining states tend to be opposed. Geographical differences always seem to amplify differences such as this when trying to develop a one-size-fits-all approach.

In the predominantly liberal parts of the country, the idea of arming teachers is considered so incongruous with local philosophy that arguments aren't even made. Arguments are made, however, against the more middle-of-the-road strategy of armed guards. In addition to cost, the limitations and risks of this approach are espoused, including the risks of accidents, the escalation of violence, the erosion of school culture, and treating children who aggress with a more punitive approach.

On the opposite side of the continuum from the NRA are civil-rights groups who don't want to see overcorrections to school violence. "While school police were intended to address threats to school safety, their role has typically devolved into addressing school discipline—with law enforcement tactics," said Matthew Cregor of the NAACP Legal Defense Fund.[2] Those tactics are more likely to be punitive as opposed to constructive, involving intimidation and threat. While a strong legal deterrence may be effective in the moment, it can also lead to more serious infractions.

Several other notable organizations have expressed reservations about armed guards in schools. The National Council of Juvenile and Family Court Judges (NCJFCJ) said "Research shows that a first-time arrest doubles the odds that a student will drop out of high school, and a first-time court appearance quadruples the odds."[3] The American Psychological Association, the Council of State Governments, and the Centers for Disease Control and Prevention all found that "Extreme discipline, including arrests; predict grade retention, school dropout, and future involvement in the juvenile and criminal justice systems. As a result, students face lasting consequences, not only in the justice system, but also when applying for college, the military, or a job."[4]

According to Judith Browne Dianis, codirector of the Advancement Project, "We cannot make our schools safer with more guns. Instead of stopping crime—which rarely happens on school grounds—the real impact of armed guards in schools is a dramatic increase in students arrested for minor misbehaviors. Children are being arrested, handcuffed, and treated as criminals for things like violating a dress code, talking back to a teacher, bringing a cell phone to school, and other minor misbehaviors that would be better solved by a counselor or a trip to the principal's office."[5]

While it may not be an entirely fair comparison due to the distinctly different population, let's look at prisons, the most common place armed guards are employed. Even with violent convicted offenders, interviews with over two dozen corrections officers unanimously report that punishment is not a way to dissuade inmates from acting violently any more than the armed guards' presence was. What the correction officers reported is that the inmates simply looked for more covert means to accomplish their objectives and if behaving violently was one of those goals, nothing was going to stop them.

We may discredit this example because prisons are filled with convicted criminals, former members of society who could not integrate themselves successfully without breaking the law. The rest of us after all have better impulse control and don't require law enforcement monitoring our every move. Or do we? We now have automatic radar monitoring for speeding, video cameras at many traffic lights, and thousands of law enforcement officers monitoring our Internet use. Are we a society of primitively evolved beings who if not for the deterrence of laws and monitors would degenerate into anarchy? If so, doesn't that advocate for a stronger presence in our schools, which are simply microcosms of our society?

The danger of having armed guards in schools is three-fold. The more obvious of the dangers is the possibility of an accident occurring, which could be irrevocable if the guard is carrying a firearm. The second risk is that which was outlined by the opposition groups citing research on recidivism and escalation of violence. The third and perhaps less obvious danger is the potential impact on school culture.

A school with an armed guard is sending a message to the students that the school is or may become unsafe, in spite of the protection offered. Why unsafe and not safer if the guard is effective at their job? The answer is that people perform according to the level of expectation.

If you enter a public restroom in a restaurant that is extremely clean and well kept, chances are better that you will take care to keep the same level of neatness as when you entered. If you enter that same restroom and see papers on the floor and dirt in the sink, you will be less likely to clean up after yourself. This is human nature to adapt to our surroundings. If we perceive something in a certain way (hold it as figural), it will influence the way we act toward that thing.

Let's consider whether the two students at Columbine would have planned and executed their plan if their school had armed guards. An argument can certainly be made that the guards may have intervened in ways that saved lives.

Perhaps the answer is best addressed while considering the different types of violence described in the first chapter. For schools in poor neighborhoods where crime is rampant, institutional violence is more likely. The presence of armed guards or security personnel may be needed to maintain order.

NOTES

1. Melanie Hunter, "NRA: Only thing that stops a bad guy with a gun is a good guy with a gun" December 21, 2012, http://cnsnews.com/news/article/nra-only-thing-stops-bad-guy-gun-good-guy-gun.

2. Jennifer Farmer and Leila McDowell, "Broad-based coalition launch campaign to oppose deployment of armed guards in schools," March 28, 2013, http://www.advancementproject.org/news/entry/broad-based-coalition-launch-campaign-to-oppose-deployment-of-armed-guards.

3. National Council of juvenile and family court judges, NCJFCJ's position on increased police presence in schools, January 15, 2013, http://www.ncjfcj.org/ncjfcjs-position-increased-police-presence-schools.

4. National Council of juvenile and family court judges, NCJFCJ's position on increased police presence in schools, January 15, 2013, http://www.ncjfcj.org/ncjfcjs-position-increased-police-presence-schools.

5. Jennifer Farmer and Leila McDowell, "Broad-based coalition launch campaign to oppose deployment of armed guards in schools" March 28, 2013, http://www.advancementproject.org/news/entry/broad-based-coalition-launch-campaign-to-oppose-deployment-of-armed-guards

TWO

Surveillance and Intelligence

A seventeen-year-old in Benton County, Oregon, named Grant Acord was arrested for plotting to detonate several bombs at West Albany High School after Memorial Day in May 2013. His plan was to execute an attack more deadly than Columbine, and according to police sources he was found with enough explosives to do just that. Had it not been for a tip to law enforcement that Acord had been making explosives, he may have been successful.

A key prevention strategy is "good surveillance and good intelligence," said Elliott, founding director of the CU-Boulder Center for the Study and Prevention of Violence. "We need to enlist our students, our teachers and our adults in the community to help us and ask them to notify the police or the sheriff if they see something unusual or have heard that something is about to happen."[1]

This approach relies on acquiring data through monitoring, leading to millions of dollars being spent in the past five years on video cameras and monitoring. From available reports to date, a high percentage of routine violations have been discovered through this process, although no known master plots have been unearthed. We may speculate from this that surveillance systems are best served to detect and discourage more routine forms of violence but are not geared toward thwarting more in-depth plots such as the recent event in Oregon.

The tragedy in Newtown, Connecticut, is a prime example, as the school had an active video-camera surveillance and a buzzer entrance system, neither of which could stop a determined killer.

The data-gathering aspect of this prevention strategy has turned personnel into monitors and investigators. A middle-school counselor in Colorado diverted an estimated 30 percent of her time to investigating reported threats and rule infractions. This means less time for dealing with crisis, counseling, and consulting with teachers. It also means a possible change in attitude toward the counselor by the students. When this counselor in Colorado now approaches students in the building, their reaction is to get tense. Instead of being seen as a support for their problems, she is now treated with suspicion and they are wary of being investigated.

Intelligence is the best prevention method for serious violence according to many in law enforcement. If it weren't for students and other community members informing law enforcement of suspicious activity, there would very likely be more deaths from incidents like the ones that have made national headlines. A prime example is the plan by two fifth-grade boys in Fort Colville Elementary School in Colville, Washington, to kill classmates. The two boys, ages ten and eleven, told authorities that they determined to murder an "annoying" classmate and were also going to kill, or "get," six more students and even identified them from a class list. Had it not been for a student's report to school personnel, they may have carried out their plan.

An important question to ask is why a student would report or not report suspicious behavior to adults or authorities. It might seem obvious as an adult that a student would want to protect themselves and their classmates, but there is more that goes into the decision-making process for a child.

Not wanting to be a rat, fearing that others wouldn't believe them, not wanting to create a false alarm and be embarrassed, not wanting to risk ostracism from their peer group, and not taking perceived threats seriously (doubting themselves) are just a few reasons that crucial information may never be relayed to law enforcement.

We can tie this into our discussion on school culture as well. Schools that are fragmented with strained relationships and a low sense of community will diminish the student's desire to protect their environment. In a school culture where taking constructive risks is avoided out of fear of punishment or embarrassment, students may learn to keep to themselves and not "stick their necks out." "Tattling" is a term used to describe peers telling on each other, although we might wonder why in some schools turning a peer in might be viewed as a healthy act where in another it's an unspoken code violation.

Back in the 1980s, a new school in New York City's suburb Staten Island had surveillance cameras installed throughout the hallways. The intention was surely to deter and address aberrant behavior, and the impact was initially felt by the incoming freshman class. Beyond a deterrence, this prevention method instilled fear among some students and a challenge to others. Rumors spread of all types of scary events that put many on high alert. While the cameras did little to enhance a feeling of comfort and safety within the school, they eventually faded into objects as unremarkable as signs or fire alarms.

NOTE

1. Peter Caughey, "School violence can be prevented, CU expert says" February 29, 2012, http://artsandsciences.colorado.edu/magazine/2012/02/school-violence-can-be-prevented-cu-expert-says/.

THREE
Metal Detectors

Following a slew of recent gun incidents, Florida's Orange County school district introduced the use of random metal-detector screenings in Orlando schools. They believe these metal detectors are important to improving safety, according to the district superintendent. The primary purpose of this prevention tool is to catch and discourage students who intend to carry weapons on school grounds. This step was a response to two recent cases of weapons found and threatened to be brought on campus.

This Florida district is one of many that have opted or are considering implementing this physical-violence-prevention strategy. According to the National Center for Education Statistics, 5.2 percent of public schools conducted random metal-detector screenings during the 2009–2010 school year. This is a 2 percent decline from the 1999–2000 school year. If we haven't seen a rise in this prevention method over the past ten years, it's reasonable to question why more schools don't have faith in this approach.

Price Middle School in Atlanta has metal detectors; however, this did not stop a fifteen-year-old student from shooting and wounding a fourteen-year-old student in a courtyard where students were moving between classes. On February 1, 2013, a student apparently evaded the school's primary deterrence system with an estimated cost of over four thousand dollars per unit, not including the high cost of operating the equipment. The message here may be that students who are determined to commit violence will not be stopped but will simply find more creative strategies to exact their vengeance. Students may actually see the physical deterrence as a challenge as opposed to an obstacle.

We might consider that the use of metal detectors is a strategy more applicable to schools with affiliative and impulsive violence. Schools where gangs are prevalent, that have a higher incidence of fights, and have a greater prevalence of weapons being carried to school, and so on, are more suitable to this physical prevention method. As opposed to the 5.2 percent of schools nationwide that use metal detectors, about 12 percent of urban high schools and 9 percent of urban middle schools utilize this approach.

If we are considering catastrophic student violence however, metal detectors may not be sufficient. Consider the students Mitchell Johnson and Andrew Golden, who sat in a field after pulling a fire alarm, opening fire on their classmates and teachers. They hid their weapons outside the school building, which any student with a moderate degree of intelligence can do to thwart metal detectors.

For the student wishing to create mass casualties, bringing a bomb that has no traces of metal would be a reasonable substitute for guns. Are we then going to have bomb-sniffing dogs at every metal detector for children to pass through?

The National Association of Secondary School Principals' (NASSP) school safety specialist, Bill Bond, said that when somebody arrives at school already shooting, metal detectors would make little difference. He notes that human error and student ingenuity will not prevent 100 percent of the weapons from being kept out of schools. "If a student wants to beat the system, students are smart enough to know how to beat the system and bypass that entrance with the metal detector," he says.[1]

Civil rights groups are concerned with schools seeming more like prisons, which is how the students may feel inside. The impact on civil liberties, the effect on school culture, and certainly the cost are all part of the controversy for this tool, which has mixed reviews of efficacy. Consider questions such as: How much time it will take to get hundreds of students through the screening and on time for class? How many security professionals will be hired to operate the detectors, impacted by full-day versus partial-day operations? If it's a partial day of operations, what about tardy students and visitors to the school? What type of training will be provided to those operating the detectors, both at the onset and on an ongoing basis? Will the school be willing to conduct tests of the staff and equipment, such as surprise inspections and undercover persons carrying concealed weapons? Will the screening only be used at the main entrance, and how will the other entry ways be secured? Will all weapons on the first floor be permanently secured so that weapons can't be passed through openings (if this is legal with fire marshals)?

There are many pragmatic questions to be answered, and still there is no guarantee that a school employing these measures will be 100 percent effective. The equipment is only as good as the people who operate it, and human error has already been noted. One school in Cleveland during a news undercover operation was found to have turned off their metal detector to speed up entry into the building. In 2008, a school in

Milwaukee with a $50,000 metal detector recently installed had a stabbing involving a fifteen-year-old student.

As with all types of prevention strategies, there is a lot to consider. One method is generally successful as part of an overall strategy and not a panacea. Schools should never implement such an expensive and involved approach as a reflexive reaction to violence.

NOTE

1. Stacy Teicher Khadaroo, "Atlanta school shooting raises doubts about metal detectors," February 1, 2013, http://www.csmonitor.com/USA/Education/2013/0201/Atlanta-school-shooting-raises-doubts-about-metal-detectors.

FOUR
Zero-Tolerance Policies

An interesting phenomenon has occurred since the tragedy at Columbine, which the media has referred to as the Columbine Effect. Because school personnel are fearful of being the next Columbine, they have begun to overreact to perceived threats and tighten their regulations into policies such as "zero tolerance." While some may view this no-nonsense approach as a constructive mechanism to combat potential violence, there is a hidden danger in terms of adaptation.

Whenever we make rules that have no bend in them, we take discretion out of the equation. We also disempower our leaders to make decisions that may call for flexibility or creativity. By maintaining a zero-tolerance policy, we also risk making outcasts of parents who feel betrayed by not having their unique situations considered. Consider the following examples of zero tolerance and judge for yourself whether the schools listed seem adaptive.

A seven-year-old boy in Cahokia, Illinois, is suspended for having a nail clipper at school. A tenth grader at Surry County High School in Virginia is kicked out for having blue-dyed hair. A Minnesota high school nixes a yearbook photo of an Army enlistee in the senior class because it shows her sitting atop a cannon outside a Veterans of Foreign Wars post. These examples were provided in an article written by John Cloud.[1] In his article he goes on to talk about the origin of zero-tolerance policies.

Kids have virtually no First or Fourth Amendment rights (guaranteeing basic civil liberties and preventing undue searches). Unless they can invoke a special circumstance, such as a mental disability, kids often have thin grounds on which to base a defense against school punishment. That's because the US Supreme Court has eroded student protections granted in the 1960s. In 1995, Justice Antonin Scalia wrote a caustic decision allowing drug testing of students. "Minors," he said, "lack some of the most fundamental rights of self-determination—including even the right of liberty in its narrow sense, i.e., the right to come and go at will."[2] The ruling was widely seen to give administrators carte blanche in punishing students, though schools still must follow some weak due-process guidelines.

Some research has been done on this topic, finding that schools employing "harsh disciplinary policies" have students who feel less safe.[3] Equate this with parents who dole out excessive punishments for behavior that could have been curtailed with a more synchronous consequence that makes sense to the child. Otherwise children may become resentful or even fearful of making mistakes, which is what this research is suggesting.

In spite of the policy's inherent disempowering influence to students who commit infractions, they have high approval in the public. Cloud reported in his article that Americans favor zero-tolerance policies overwhelmingly, which is all the schools need to know to enact and maintain such measures. This is quite understandable as there is no guesswork involved for administrators. There is a feeling of safety that comes with addressing each questionable act as a punishable threat to the school environment.

There is a reason that the United States has the highest rates of incarceration in the world.

Two-thirds of the people who get out of prison will commit another crime. If recidivism is this high, we can safely estimate that punishment is not an effective means of deterring behavior. So where is the value of expelling a student from school who demonstrates poor behavior? Is there any chance students like this are going to become model citizens if they are rejected by school and enter adulthood with no education? For those who have already suffered in their lives, this could be experienced as further abandonment.

This doesn't mean that one unruly student should diminish the climate for the rest of the student body. There is also an argument to be made for setting an example of one student to alert the others that gross violations will not be tolerated. While punishment may not be an effective deterrent for that particular youth, perhaps it would serve as a behavior modifier for those on the periphery. If this policy is used, however, leaders may be tempted to apply the punishment as a means of gaining control over the school, even in instances where the behavior may have been borderline severe or even less.

Administrators have been known to apply this policy to written or oral expression, which falls outside the scope of its original intention. Writer Ari Paul named this "subzero tolerance," and included behaviors such as writing in a journal about a deranged student going on a rampage.[4] Such was the case for Antonius Brown in Atlanta, who was suspended for twenty days.

There is an argument to be made in favor of strict policies, which parallels the issue going on in Major League Baseball. Back in the 1990s when illegal performance-enhancing drugs were rampant, many players, including some very famous ones, engaged in this practice in spite of the rules. They did so in part because they believed they could get away with it and neither the severity nor consistency of applied consequences were enough to deter them. Now, as the commissioner of baseball has consistently enforced very harsh consequences for this rule violation, the attitude of violating the rules is shifting. The players who are abiding by the rules are putting pressure on those who aren't and are not covering up for them as they did in the past. Could all this be a direct result of stricter enforcement, and, if so, doesn't that mean zero-tolerance policies in schools can be effective?

NOTES

1. John Cloud, "The Columbine Effect," *Time*, November 28, 1999, http://content.time.com/time/magazine/article/0,9171,35098,00.html.
2. Scalia, *Vernonia School District v. Action*, June 26, 1995, http://www.supremecourthistory.org/learning-center/we-the-students/vernonia-school-district/.
3. Patricia E. Hudson, R. Craig Windham, and Lisa M. Hooper, "Characteristics of School Violence and the Value of Family-School Therapeutic Alliances," *Journal of School Violence* 4, no. 2 (2005): 133–46.
4. A. Paul, posted on http://www.umich.edu/~michind/83/counter_revolution.html.

FIVE
Peer Mediation

In 1984, about three dozen educators and practitioners met in Cape Cod for the first conference on what eventually was named Peer Mediation. Without any quantitative research to support their beliefs, young people across the nation's schools were being trained in an approach that a decade later spread across the United States and Canada, and eventually the world.

Peer-mediation programs present today are either cadre or total-student-body programs. In the *cadre approach*, a small number of students are trained to serve as peer mediators for the entire school. This approach is relatively simple and inexpensive to implement; it means that students throughout the school are not learning how to become better negotiators of conflict.

Cadre programs are popular in schools because they take the burden off of administrators and teachers. Aside from the designated adult responsible for training and overseeing the mediators and the program itself, most educators in the schools remain uninvolved, allowed to focus on other work. Serving in the program also serves as a reward for students who have achieved either socially or academically, potentially influencing others to elevate their own efforts.

If done well, peer mediators can work well in middle and elementary schools so long as those responsible for facilitating the meetings are well trained. Young people tend to listen more to other young people, providing a social influencing component that adults aren't capable of. Young mediators may also be more likely to take seriously the issues being brought to the table, unlike adults who might be tempted to minimize what seem to be trivial matters.

The limitations of peer-mediation programs are potentially serious. If a young mediator, who is already under a fair amount of pressure to be helpful, fails to keep those involved from building their resentments, conflicts can graduate. Most peer mediators have an adult present to help oversee the process, but this doesn't mean the adult can detect when participants are being agreeable for the sake of aesthetics as opposed to being genuinely satisfied with the outcome.

Additionally, students throughout the school are not learning how to improve their own conflict-resolution skills. Having a handful of mediators in the school does very little for the hundreds of others who don't feel confident to request mediation, aren't identified by an adult or student to qualify for mediation, or are too bitter to pursue this option. Mediation can work well for those who are willing but fail miserably for those who are never identified.

An even scarier notion is the idea of the potential school shooter, who has often been known as a recluse or nondescript individual, unlikely to get into any overt conflicts with peers. This inward student may be bottling up hostility in a way that doesn't show up in the day-to-day skirmishes many students encounter. These are the students for whom a peer-mediation program may do little good.

If the peer-mediation program were more geared toward teaching the entire student body how to manage conflicts constructively, and the designated peer mediators served as facilitators for a process that is being learned school-wide, there may be a greater advantage. Or even if the responsibility for becoming a peer mediator is rotated throughout the entire student body, so each child had time to serve as a process catalyst, greater value may be generated.

Teaching Students to Be Peacemakers (TSP) is a school-based program that teaches conflict-resolution procedures and peer-mediation skills throughout the entire school. The program's chief objective is to create a supportive school community where differences are addressed peaceably. Students learn to be peacemakers in four steps, beginning with a normative view of conflict as healthy and desirable. Next, they learn how to negotiate what they term "integrative agreements" to conflicts, which conclude in a plan of action for both parties. Third, students are taught how to mediate peer conflicts, to assume a greater stake in the school community. Last, teachers implement the peer-mediation component in which each student gets experience serving as a mediator.

Ultimately, the program assumes that greater self-regulation is critical for cognitive and social development, allowing students to cope more effectively with stress and adversity. Thus the locus of control becomes internal, as opposed to external, as would be the case with a small group of mediators whose job it was to resolve the immediate issue.

SIX
Antibullying Campaigns

Over the past decade we have spawned hundreds of antibullying programs at every level of primary and secondary education. These programs range in depth and scope, strategy and philosophy, and even cost per duration. They are age specific, ranging from early childhood to late adolescence. They can be workshops done online, teacher taught, or administered by an outside consultant or professional.

Let's Be Friends is an early childhood education program designed to discourage bullying. This is a rather typical program in that it covers areas including friendship, kindness, differences, and reporting. The program is geared for both children and parents, with reinforcing activities to do at home. And while this program seems to cover some important bases, there are several potential problems.

First, the schools that tend to need these programs the most are the least likely to employ them. Second, if the program is administered but there isn't any follow-up, or the school culture doesn't support healthy relationships among the faculty, the program will lose effectiveness. Last, the parents whose children need this program the most are also the least likely to do the follow-up exercises at home.

Some of the same concerns exist for a middle-school program called Stand Up–Speak Out. This program has some differences in that it targets bystanders more, in particular when it comes to cyberbullying. It also helps children not be a target of bullying, which may only be a fraction of what it would take to prevent this from occurring. Kids who are the targets for bullies have identities that have already solidified by this point in time, which helps them to seem vulnerable to bullies. While this program does encourage projects done by students in the school, it does nothing to address the culture in which the program or projects are executed.

The Olweus Bullying Prevention Program (OBPP) claims to be the most researched and best-known bullying-prevention program available today. The emphasis of the program is peer relationships and how students can better negotiate differences that lead to bullying. The limitation of this program, as others, is the limited attention it pays to the organization as a whole. If bullying is going on in school, there is a high likelihood the environment created in large part by adult relationships is not as constructive as it could be. Helping children to work through their differences more effectively when adults are witnessed and experienced as fragmented will seem hypocritical to those targeted.

A review of existing bullying-prevention programs, including the Olweus Program, by Dr. Jonathan Cohen, PhD and others concluded that its efficacy is questionable. They report that OBPP is no longer on the Substance Abuse and Mental Health Services Administration (SAMSHA) National Registry of Evidence-Based Programs (www.nrepp.samhsa.gov); however is still endorsed by the National Educational Association.

StopBullying.gov is a website created by the US Department of Health and Human Services. There are quite a few problems with this website that may limit its efficacy, beginning with the "prevent at school" page, which offers a very broad outline of what the school can do. One sentence suggesting the school create a safe environment with "positive climate" is too vague. It's important that it was mentioned because it means that legislators are aware of the link between bullying and school culture, so this is something that can be built upon. More specific ideas, references, links to consultants, and tutorial videos are all needed to bolster this message.

The same can be said for the other categories they have on this page, including assessing bullying, which is an enormously complex undertaking. Assessing bullying can't be done by looking at statistics because many incidents go unreported. Evaluating bullying must include attention to attitudes, relationships (both students with students, students with faculty, faculty with faculty, faculty with administration, and administration with students). This doesn't even include relationships with parents and the community.

The results of recent meta-analyses for bullying-prevention programs show little to no effectiveness in either reducing victimization or decreasing aggressive behavior. A review of sixteen studies over a twenty-five-year period and fifteen thousand students on two continents found positive effect for only one-third of the study variables, which were limited to knowledge, attitude, and perceptions of bullying but not the actual bullying itself.

The extensive review of bullying-prevention programs by Dr. Jonathan Cohen and associates concluded with explanations for why bullying-prevention programs are limited. First, most bullying-prevention programs are not grounded in educational, developmental, or psychological theory. Second, most programs do not encourage collaboration for a shared vision of what students and educators want their community to look like. It's not enough to say, "Reduce bullying!" if there is no effort to consider where the school would like to evolve to. Third, most programs fail to address the ecology that promotes and sustains bullying. Fourth, many evaluations of these programs do not address socioeconomic influences and other community demographics. Fifth, many programs fail to capture underlying risk factors associated with persistent aggression. Sixth, these programs often require resources such as funding and teacher time, both of which are in short supply. Seventh, bullying does not only occur among students, as teachers are both the recipients and antagonists in this dynamic, and we must also include parents in the equation. Eighth and finally, the implementation of many programs does not tailor strategy to the unique ecology of each school.

SEVEN

Mental-Health Specialists

The Secret Service published a report in 2002 titled *The Safe School Initiative: Implications for the Prevention of School Attacks in the United States.*[1] This report was a research project studying thirty-seven incidents of catastrophic school violence in the years between 1974 and 2000. This was a joint initiative between the US Department of Education and the Secret Service, looking for key characteristics of established attackers to help identify the potential profile for future perpetrators.

The Safe School Initiative report has led to at least one specific change in the way one state deals with prevention, which takes seriously the findings that many shooters were known by others to be in distress prior to the event. The state of Delaware's school system spent three million dollars in 2013 to hire thirty mental health professionals, each of whom earned a salary of $80,000 to monitor students in school. These trained specialists monitored student behavior to help identify significant problems before they might escalate into something dramatic.

This is the first intervention of this type in the country, with a sizable budget and specific staff being brought on with the sole purpose of school violence prevention. They are working off the premise that students show warning signs if we are paying attention that can be an indication of something more serious. The state also plans on expanding their community mental health outreach in order to provide needed intervention services for at-risk youth.

There are some important benefits to creating this type of prevention approach, the most significant of which is recognizing that students are dealing with emotional issues that interfere with their academics and discipline alone cannot fix. Having mental health professionals in the building may mean that students will have more options for seeking support or be attended to even without their taking initiative. This can be helpful for students who are less likely to go to a guidance counselor or be recognized as troubled by their teachers.

In spite of the sincere effort by lawmakers and district administrators, this approach has several limitations that require consideration: (1) This is an expensive experimental method of attempting to prevent violence that has no proven results. Since the national income-to-expense ratio of the average US school is $611,000 to $623,000, they are already operating in a deficit. (2) This method does not tap into the wealth of valuable information available to the school by involving educators who see children on a regular basis. How will essays, homework assignments, classroom observations, and other data available only in the classroom be obtained? (3) The mental health professionals in the school will not necessarily know what to look for because it isn't clearly established that we are looking for fluid, not static, traits. It's patterns of behavior over time that create the red flags and not just problematic recent behavior, which means utilizing relationships with students over a period of time. (4) This will not help students who transfer districts or change schools within the district. With the number of students who change schools, more anecdotal information is needed to create a system of continuity. (5) This approach doesn't address other factors such as school culture, which is an important contextual component for school violence.

The idea is taking us in a good direction, recognizing that we need to identify youth in trouble and not allow them to flounder in their own discontent. Hopefully, the school district will compile data on this new approach to help us better understand the efficacy of this intervention.

NOTE

1. B. Vossekuil, R. Fein, M. Reddy, R. Borum, and W. Modzeleski, *Final Report and Findings of the Safe School Initiative: Implications for the Prevention of School Attacks in the United States*, US Department of Education, Office of Elementary and Secondary Education, Safe and Drug-Free Schools Program, and US Secret Service, National Threat Assessment Center, Washington, D.C., 2002.

EIGHT

Threat-Assessment Teams

Because of the complexity of the school shooter portfolio, educational institutions as well as other public and private organizations are turning to consulting groups for assistance. These consulting groups generally consist of a combination of law-enforcement, legal, and forensic professionals who can either train staff in the school or serve as an external resource for the purpose of violence prevention and intervention.

Training, consultation, and support are the three services often provided to districts that can afford this assistance. These three services include policy review, team building, climate surveys, case review, and coaching. In essence, schools are being helped to become more attuned to potential dangers, similar to the way a secret service agent might anticipate threats to the president.

Sigma Threat Management Associates is one such group that trains schools how to identify, investigate, assess, and intervene in cases of threats and other concerning behavior. They help schools take a more proactive and preventive stance to protect students and faculty to manage threatening situations before they can escalate. On their team is the former secret service agent, who along with other active and retired law-enforcement professionals created a research document *Prior Knowledge of School Based Violence,* assessing what information students may have to prevent attacks (http://www.secretservice.gov/ntac/bystander_study.pdf.).

This is a relatively new violence-prevention strategy and hasn't yet been adequately assessed through research to determine its efficacy. Due to the options for insourcing versus outsourcing, along with the different services available and the number of companies that are beginning to do this work, it may be difficult to validate.

There are several potential limitations to this approach. The most evident is a consistent issue with all existing prevention programs, which is the contextual element. While these threat-assessment groups sometimes offer to measure school climate, there are questions as to the reliability and validity of the assessment tools. Not everybody uses the same instruments to measure school culture, and not everybody who is measuring school culture is looking at the same variables. Most in fact are taking a segment of school culture—in this book referred to as "school climate"—whereas "culture" is much broader and more diverse than most account for.

Another limitation is the quality of the training for the threat-assessment teams is going to vary according to the trainer. There will also be variability according to the faculty members who are being trained and their skill levels. The market is growing for training on this topic, not heard of ten years prior. The services help train staff, develop relationships with local law enforcement, and develop safety plans for "what if" scenarios.

Ron Stephens, PhD, has been the executive director of the National School Safety Center (NSSC) for nearly thirty years. NSSC was established in 1984 by a presidential directive and serves as a resource for school districts internationally.

Dr. Stephens has helped administrators from many of the nation's schools victimized by school violence including Columbine; Red Lake, Minnesota; and Paducha, Kentucky. In his conversations with these school leaders, he has consistently heard how unprepared they were for the crisis they faced. For this reason, Dr. Stephens urges schools everywhere to not be caught unprepared by planning now for worst-case scenarios, before it's too late.

Threat-assessment protocols are vital according to Dr. Stephens, who believes an effective crisis plan includes a mutual aid plan with first responders as well as leadership training and technical assistance for schools that need it. For many schools, a more comprehensive assessment of vulnerabilities is needed because they are not designed for this level of protection.

NINE
Restorative Justice

Schools are following the trend in society to deal with rule violations through stricter punishments including expulsions, suspensions, surveillance, and partnerships with law enforcement agencies; however, this may in fact reinforce aggression and other behavioral problems. An alternative to this model of prevention is derived from the model of restorative justice, which focuses on repairing the harm caused by the offense and community participation in disciplinary procedures.

Restorative justice principles extend beyond the aftermath of misconduct into the early stages of conflict resolution and remediation. Schools across the country and in other parts of the world are using this philosophy of early intervention as a forum where anybody can address problems in their earliest stages of development. The goal is to improve the school's capacity to deal with adversity and conflict, which can promote greater adaptation in the school culture.

The restorative justice system has been utilized in several schools with high percentages of disadvantaged youth, promoting social skill development and constructive conflict-resolution opportunities, and finds greater success in reducing disciplinary problems of all types.

According to the executive director, Dr. Fania Davis, Restorative Justice for Oakland Youth's (RJOY) own program in West Oakland's Cole Middle School eliminated violence and expulsions and reduced the rate of suspensions by more than 75 percent. She pointed to a 2009 study by the International Institute for Restorative Practices (IIRP)[1] that found schools implementing restorative practices from six schools located in communities in Pennsylvania, ranging from urban to rural and impoverished to middle class. As was the case at Cole Middle School, all six schools in this study witnessed significant drops in suspensions, expulsions, disruptive behavior, reoffending, violence, and discipline referrals generally.

A West Philadelphia teacher reported feeling less aggressive after shifting her classroom to a circle instead of the traditional student-facing-teacher alignment, reportedly building a sense of family among her students. As part of a movement toward restorative practices, this same district reported significant decreases in crime and violence after implementing this approach. They even applied the concept to students who were unhappy with a teacher and because this teacher allowed herself to be vulnerable, the meeting was highly productive.

Restorative justice has been used in schools by countries around the world with similar reported success. New Zealand's juvenile justice system adopted a nationwide, family-focused restorative approach in 1989 and boasts a nearly crime-free community with detention centers being shut down.

Dr. Davis and others in the movement are working through the natural resistance of educators and community members who are hesitant to be a part of this process. It can feel threatening for a teacher to acknowledge aloud that her reaction to a student was in part generated by previous trauma, but doing so creates a strong bond between adults and students that create corrective emotional experiences for everybody involved. Students learn to trust adults and work through some of the tremendous obstacles put in their path, such as parents with alcoholism.

Dr. Davis also believes that talking circles and other restorative justice methods can be used proactively to prevent traumatic cycles from repeating and even intensifying into punitive reactions by adults. A simple extension of caring about why a child is reacting can interrupt a downward spiral from ending badly. A child who gets into a heated argument with a teacher can quickly degenerate into suspension and even police involvement, whereas the underlying issue may be problems going on at home. If the child isn't provoked into a power struggle, an adult can deescalate the situation by looking deeper into the cause of the disturbance. When the circle commences, each person is asked to take ownership of their part and work toward a resolution, both at that time and for the future.

If retributive violence is rooted in retributive justice, a case can be made for restorative justice as the remedy. Instead of a system that promotes punishment, influencing young people to exact vengeance, a remediation process that encourages healing may teach a more constructive lesson. This approach will need to be explored outside of a select number of mostly inner-city schools in the United States, dealing with more impulsive and affiliative violence. Retributive violence may be more a product of overly homogenous schools of mostly middle-class students who don't experience potential aggression on a daily basis. There is less competition for resources in these middle-class schools and a less rapid escalation of conflicts, eliciting different responses from students and educators.

The use of circles in particular has long been associated with balance and connectivity. In a system, what one person does affects everybody else in the system, which is well represented in circles that hold each person accountable for both cause and solution. Having educators on the same plane as students, willing to look at their part as a way to promote accountability, is an idea that can be incorporated into any system that is open enough to accept it. Relationships with children require a delicate balance between being accessible versus setting limits, requiring constant vigilance in managing this process, which requires something simple and meaningful to students that they can both understand and embrace.

Restorative justice reminds us that punishment is different from consequences. Punishment typically belittles and frightens children but doesn't promote learning based on internalized rules and values. Consequences, primarily those that are natural, logical, related, and born out of empathy and negotiation, can teach children valuable lessons that are more self-sustaining.

NOTE

1. "Restorative Practices in Educational Settings, Whole-School Change Program," www.SaferSanerSchools.org.

TEN
Overview and Conclusions

Current strategies for preventing violence in schools are wide ranging. As a group they seem to be pragmatic, action oriented, and often controversial. Many programs lack ongoing support, have questionable fits with the school system, and don't always have the backing of validity testing. Overall, the state of prevention efforts in our nation's schools seems varied in a way that makes it confusing for officials to select from and often times only address certain issues that influence the potential for violence in that school.

Because the causes of violence are diverse, the strategies to inhibit these causes must match. If we apply a single cause across the nine different types of violence, there is a good chance we will fall short. When we consider retributionist or cyclonic violence, we must be multidimensional in our conception of the issue. Traditional approaches that are strictly programmatic or one-dimensional may fall short and be short-lived.

We might consider whether bullying-prevention programs need to be absorbed into violence-prevention programs or if the dynamics of this particular type of intimidation violence need to be addressed uniquely. It is generally agreed upon by industry experts that a combination of risk and protective factors need to be a part of any approach to decreasing the risk of violence, much like we would use rewards and consequences to help train our own children. Building on existing strengths while targeting limitations provides a more well-balanced approach.

As for the more specific strategies that deal with the infrastructure of the school, such as surveillance, armed guards, and zero-tolerance policies, we want to consider them on a case-by-case basis. An inner-city school in Camden is going to warrant a different violence-prevention program than a rural school in Mississippi.

If we consider violence/bullying prevention as one entity, we want to include all the best features of existing prevention programs while attending to the other influences, such as community, school culture, and familial and student dynamics. Some states have already begun to think along these lines, but implementation is not yet congruent with philosophy. Let's take a look at one of the more progressive states and the ideology developed around violence prevention.

The New York Office of Mental Health developed a guideline for violence-prevention strategies to help mediate the risk factors of violence in schools. It's worthwhile to review these guidelines because they are broader in scope than more targeted bullying-prevention programs often are.

They advocate developing "protective" factors that counter some of the risk factors associated with violence. Being proactive in building healthy students is similar to the traditional parenting techniques that help children better manage their feelings as opposed to focusing entirely on discipline. Some of the categories they focus on are individual, school-wide, and district-wide.

Individual characteristics they aim to build include resiliency, even temperament, being good-natured, and enjoying social interactions. They also promote strong relationships with family members, teachers, or other adults.

The guidelines address the importance of adults becoming role models to demonstrate success without violence. Adults are encouraged to reach out to students to help them feel cared for. Tutors are encouraged from the school or community to build relationships with adults, which may also lead to volunteerism and part-time employment. Getting involved with community events builds a sense of investment in one's community, which can also deter violence.

The school-wide strategies are intended to help youths develop tools to manage conflict nonviolently through avenues such as:

- Anger-management and counseling programs
- Mediation and conflict-resolution programs
- A confidential reporting system for youth to alert school personnel with concerns regarding peers, stressing the differences between "ratting" and being safe
- Alcohol and drug interventions for youths and their families
- Links with youth-serving and law-enforcement agencies in the community
- Extended school hours for organized recreation activities, childcare, and so on
- Classes for parenting skills
- In-school crisis centers, staffed by professionals to work with violent youths and to be used as a "cooling off" space

- A crisis team consisting of teachers, administrators, and other school personnel
- Training on managing violent youths for all school personnel
- Monitoring by staff and guards
- Parents as monitors or teachers aids
- Discipline and dress codes
- Zero-tolerance policies
- A Post-incident Response Plan as part of the Incident Management Plan
- Mental health staff available to provide consultation and counseling to students, school personnel, and the community immediately after a crisis and on its anniversary dates
- Self-help networks for students and their families who have survived a crisis

Their idea for district-wide strategies amount solely to an ongoing review and revision of discipline codes that comply with federal, state, and local education laws. They encourage schools to use graduated sanctions that are enforced consistently and firmly.

It seems from the list that there is a strong emphasis on discipline, including zero-tolerance policies, a dress code, and guards, perhaps a reflection of having so many inner-city schools that deal with more impulsive and affiliative violence.

The one component missing from these guidelines, however, is attention to the health of the school. If a school has a culture that promotes subgrouping and incongruence between mission/vision and policies/procedure, the effect of these guidelines may be confusing. The confidential reporting system, for instance, may not be utilized because there is fear of retribution, with students not trusting the adults to keep their reports confidential.

From the state to the national level, the Centers for Disease Control (CDC) has a section on their website dedicated to school violence prevention. They echo the notion that violence evolves from an often complex set of factors requiring adaptive and synchronous tactics. Their website specifies, "No one factor in isolation causes school violence, so stopping school violence involves using multiple prevention strategies that address the many individual, relationship, community, and societal factors that influence the likelihood of violence." The site goes on to affirm the importance of considering school culture: "School violence can be prevented. Research shows that prevention efforts—by teachers, administrators, parents, community members, and even students—can reduce violence and improve the overall school environment."[1]

In response to the more traditional strategies described early in this chapter, the CDC writes that insufficient data on metal detectors and other security measures exists to determine their benefits, and some evidence suggests that they may negatively impact students' perceptions of safety.

The CDC suggests looking at individual-, relational-, community-, and societal-level strategies, supporting the idea that violence is multifaceted. Let's take a look at each of these four categories to see what's emphasized. The following is largely direct transcript from their site, which is important to consider as they are the national specialists in violence prevention.

Individual-level strategies include attention to problem solving, involvement in prosocial activities, emotional regulation, conflict resolution, and teamwork. Relationship-level strategies include improvement of social skills of students and intervention skills for teachers. There is an emphasis on teaching educators effective ways to manage a classroom, resolve conflicts nonviolently, promote positive relationships between students with diverse backgrounds, and create positive student–teacher relationships so that students feel comfortable talking with teachers about violence-related issues. The relationship level also includes parents by promoting family cohesion and communication-skills building.

Community-level strategies include supporting effective classroom-management practices, promoting cooperative-learning techniques, providing educators with training and support to better meet the diverse needs of students, providing opportunities to actively engage families, and creating open communication and decision-making processes. In addition to the social environment of a school, research suggests that the physical environment can influence fear and safety. Other strategies include creating a warm and welcoming environment with prominently displayed student artwork and the school's mascot/logo and by maintaining the building and parking areas by removing graffiti and making sure areas are well-lit.

The characteristics of the community surrounding schools also influence the likelihood and type of school violence. By integrating prevention efforts in schools with their surrounding communities, there is a greater chance of creating safer extended environments. Some effective community-level strategies include providing youth with more structured and supervised afterschool opportunities, such as mentoring programs or recreational activities, in order to increase monitoring and healthy skill development of youth.

The Center for the Study and Prevention of Violence in Boulder, Colorado, was established to bridge the gap between research and practice to ensure that the best that is known from violence-prevention research gets into the hands of those who need it most. To help schools, policy makers and human-service practitioners sift through the myriad of program choices. The center, through their Blueprints for Healthy Youth Development Initiative, has done the work of substantiating the merits of each program to ensure it is grounded in evidence. The Blueprints mission is to identify and disseminate evidence-based prevention and intervention programs that are effective in reducing antisocial behavior and promoting a healthy course of youth development. Blueprints evaluates the scientific merit and effectiveness of social programs, offering a Consumer Reports–type ranking of what works best. The evaluations serve as a resource for governmental agencies, foundations, and community organizations trying to make informed decisions about their investments in these types of programs. Blueprints focuses on violence and drug-use outcomes as well as mental and physical health, self-regulation, and educational achievement outcomes. Blueprints' standards for certifying model and promising programs are widely recognized as the most rigorous in use.

According to the director, Dr. Beverly Kingston, it's imperative that districts use data on risk and protective factors, school climate, and problem behaviors as a basis for selecting evidence-based prevention programs that fit both the school and community and then closely consider how the program is implemented to ensure maximum gain. Rather than choosing a program simply based on cost or convenience, Dr. Kingston recommends schools in partnership with communities create a systematic prevention infrastructure beginning in early childhood that supports healthy youth development throughout the life course—in other words, from cradle to career.

To do this, the school and community must begin by having a clear understanding of the risk and protective factors that relate to violence and other problem behaviors across multiple contexts including community, family, school, peer, and individual. The next step is to collect data on these risk and protective factors that can help schools and communities prioritize when and how to intervene using proven programs and strategies. Effective implementation is critical to ensuring the programs are delivered as intended. School and community leaders should continue to collect data on the risk and protective factors as well as the behavioral outcomes to determine if the programs and strategies being implemented are making a difference.

Societal-level strategies looks at the broader social and cultural climate that surrounds schools affecting the likelihood of school violence. By creating the conditions and systems to put evidence-based violence-prevention approaches in place, violence experienced by school-aged youth can be decreased. Examples of this work include prioritizing prevention and the use of public-health strategies that are based on the best available evidence. Addressing social norms about the acceptability of violence in schools and ensuring that educational systems promote strong educational growth for all students are additional strategies.

With the CDC, a sizable part of the government, advocating a diverse and broad-based approach to violence prevention based on extensive research, it's fair to question why Congress hasn't supported their findings with legislation. In fact the opposite is true. An *Education Week* analysis of more than 450 bills related to school safety filed since the deadliest K–12 school shooting in US history found that legislators have proposed solutions that include arming teachers, adding guards or police officers, and shoring up the security of school buildings. There are zero bills related to school culture.

Dr. Jonathan Cohen, a member of President Obama's task force on bullying and president of the National School Climate Center, is encouraged by the growing collaboration of state and national government. He has witnessed the emergence of cooperative planning between researchers, strategists, and policy makers more so now than at any time in the past. He believes the consensus is growing that school climate needs to be the core of every prevention campaign, building upon less effective quick-fix solutions being utilized today.

The National School Climate Center, established in 1996, advocates the focus of school climate as the foundation of effective school reform. Transformation is the central theme of the center, engaging all people to be colearners and coleaders. The center starts with three basic questions—what kind of school is desired, what are the actual strengths and weaknesses to build from, and what kind of improvement goals are desired to be worked on together. Essentially the school is helped to create a shared picture with heightened awareness of what is and what can be.

Although this center is relatively recent in existence, the ideas are not. Researchers and practitioners have been advocating a systems approach to school improvement for decades; however, this more complex and comprehensive approach did not gain traction until more recently. Understanding what others have been advocating over time can help us to avoid reinventing the wheel.

In order to better understand where we are headed, it helps to look backward in time, since this is neither the beginning of these questions nor the answer. Looking beyond statistics, it's important to question whether we have made any progress in understanding the etiology of student violence and whether that understanding has led to any worthwhile results.

An article written nearly two decades ago seems to still hold true for evaluating the efficacy of violence-prevention programs, highlighting the major pitfalls. David Johnson and Roger Johnson wrote an article in the *Journal of Educational Leadership* called "Why Violence Prevention Programs Don't Work—And What Does."[2] This was a tremendous review of the existing prevention programs, identifying the inherent weaknesses of each and the critical issues that anybody considering implementation should consider.

They begin by recognizing that schools are continuously dealing with conflicts at every level, most notably among the students. They reasonably argue that if schools are to be peaceful places promoting high-quality education, students must learn to manage conflicts constructively without physical or verbal violence. This ties into the concept of constructive differencing that can either build a cohesive community or be a precursor to violence, if poorly navigated.

The article cites the lack of evidence for long-term changes in violent behavior or risk of victimization for a majority of prevention programs at that time. They contend that anger-management and social-skills training are insufficient and that deeper conflict-resolution skills are needed. They also believed that some school prevention programs actually influenced the students to become more violence-prone, helping us to appreciate the gravity of selecting the right program. An important reason cited by the authors for schools using these evidence-lacking programs was to provide political cover for schools and politicians.

Here it is, two decades later, and we may still fall into similar pitfalls. Schools may be making decisions about violence-prevention strategies based on partial information, and still influenced by public perception. If a prevention program has a popular name attached to it or has been recommended by a neighboring school, it may still be lacking in adequacy for the unique needs of that institution.

Because of the abundance of prevention programs in existence today, it's reasonable to ask whether they work and will work for a particular school. This same article written two decades ago found that there was no clear evidence that the programs they studied produced changes in violent behavior or decreased the risk of victimization. In their study of fifty-one violence-prevention programs, fewer than half had any evidence or even made claims that they could or would reduce violence. Some programs they found even influenced nonviolent students to be more violence-prone.

The authors of this article put forth a number of suggestions as to why the violence prevention programs weren't effective; all of these reasons can still be applied to many efforts today.

Violence prevention programs (1) are not one size fits all, as violence occurs for different reasons, (2) miss the core issues of this small group of children who are prone to violence, (3) don't focus enough on implementation, providing educators too little training on the ideology and practice that support the program, (4) lack sophistication, not recognizing that violence is complex in nature, and (5) have unrealistic expectations around the social forces that impel or compel children toward violence.

The authors went beyond their critique of existing programs at the time; they also provided guidelines, both pragmatic and philosophical, for future program developments to consider. Their most emphatic suggestion is that schools focus on conflict, not to eliminate it but to help students manage it more effectively. They recognized that conflict can serve a valuable role in the school with regard to achievement, retention, reasoning, social/cognitive development, promoting resilience, self-awareness, fun, and enriching relationships.

While working to manage conflict more effectively, these programs are least effective when they simply attempt to change student behavior. The authors recognized two decades ago that the key was to "transform the total school environment into a learning community in which students live by a credo of nonviolence."

Dr. Howard Adelman is a professor of psychology at UCLA and codirector of the School Mental Health Project and Center for Mental Health in Schools. For decades, the center has pursued fundamentally new directions for student and learning supports including a number of initiatives at state departments of education and school districts that are moving forward with development of a Unified and Comprehensive System of Learning Supports.

The center's policy and practice analyses believe many well-intended advocates arguing for schools and communities to expand their role in addressing child and adolescent problems are actually counterproductive. They stress that too often the result is to further fragment a system that has sparse resources, further marginalizing efforts to address problems with respect to school improvement policy and practice.

Dr. Adelman and his codirector, Dr. Taylor, worry about the trend to add more "needs assessments," which they argue keep teacher and student support staff from becoming proactive with respect to pursuing activity that will enable a positive school climate to emerge and in some cases may lower morale. They believe school climate is an emergent quality and that it is through system building that we can best contribute to improving the culture and climate of schools.

Transforming schools into more effective and safer learning environments includes many aspects of each of the approaches outlined by the aforementioned experts. We might consider that each approach has its own merits but may ultimately achieve similar results if the basic principles of sustainable organizational change are adhered to.

The key points are that programs are research driven, theoretically grounded, sustainable with ongoing support, and well incorporated into the school culture. How schools go about selecting the right prevention approach will be based in part on familiarity/availability but also on which particular tack fits best with their own philosophy. If we consider prevention a part of learning as opposed to a specific program to offer, we will be more likely to incorporate this idea into the fabric of the school.

In addition, prevention must be inclusive of all three dimensions of school culture (adaptation, climate, infrastructure), improve the way students learn to approach conflict, and raise awareness around the complexity of violence as essential features of an effective prevention paradigm. Because few, if any, programs offer this type of comprehensive approach to making schools safer, we want to remain aware of the limitations of whatever prevention strategy a school employs while remaining vigilant around key processes that determine the needs of each school.

Furthermore, prevention efforts must be grounded in theory. If we consider existing prevention programs and efforts in the context of gestalt theory, we see a significant deficit. Consider a student who feels marginalized, belittled, and without hope who has recently experienced trauma at home, compounding an already exaggerated sense of powerlessness. If this student experiences the school culture as oppressive to the point where he imagines destructive fantasy, what are the chances a program aimed at improving conflict resolution will be successful?

An effective prevention paradigm begins with a more comprehensive exploration of the subjective experience of the child. Once we know how the students perceive their peers, teachers, administration, and school as a whole, the better chance we have of making contact with students before they vilify the school as a whole. Understanding students at a core level will lead to stronger relationships, which encourage ownership and action instead of blame and contempt.

NONVIOLENCE

Perhaps as important as improving school culture, teaching constructive differencing, or any other prevention strategy outlined in this book is the philosophy of nonviolence. Theories and practice of nonviolence are extensive in literature around the world, including by early theorists such as Lao Tzu and the unknown author of the *Bhagavad Gita*, which influenced Thoreau, who in turn had a major impact on Tolstoy, Gandhi, and Martin Luther King.

Jainism, Buddhism, Islam, and Judaism have all produced some of the historically relevant doctrines that favor nonviolence. The Dhammapada, the Talmud, and the Quran have all defined the nature and practice of peaceful living, through different ideologies and methodologies, none of which are studied in a way to incorporate the teachings into the majority of American schools.

If we are going to develop schools that are truly free of violence, we want to begin an early curriculum that brings the work of these theories into current practice. If schools can become the pioneers for American society in not just living but believing in peaceful coexistence, then the paradigms and practices outlined in this book will be more easily adapted. The philosophies around nonviolence are inspiring if we take the time to consider the deep meaning postulated in their work, which can not only help schools reshape their culture but also produce students who can do the same for society.

QUESTIONS TO CONSIDER

1. What existing prevention strategies or programs is your school using currently?
2. What are the benefits and limitations of your existing prevention approach?
3. How well does your existing prevention incorporate organizational health improvement?
4. Is your existing prevention program grounded in theory?
5. How much investment do your faculty, student body, parents, and community have in the prevention approach?
6. How well does the approach balance the physical and emotional safety of the students and faculty?

NOTES

1. The Centers for Disease Control and Prevention, "School Violence: Prevention" December 30, 2013, http://www.cdc.gov/violenceprevention/youthviolence/schoolviolence/prevention.html.

2. David W. Johnson and Roger T. Johnson, "Why Violence Prevention Programs Don't Work—And What Does," *Journal of Educational Leadership: School Reform: What We've Learned*, 52, no. 5 (1995): 63–68.

Section II

Building a Prevention Paradigm

ELEVEN
Theory and Violence Prevention

When building a paradigm for violence prevention, a theory of human behavior is needed to build the platform of our approach. Too often strategy is put before philosophy, leading to short-sighted implementation that's expensive and ineffectual. Similar to the shortcomings of traditional professional development, violence prevention that isn't grounded in established constructs will be limited.

A theory of human behavior is a lens through which we understand and make meaning of a person in their actions and interactions with others and the world. If we hope to effectively intervene either proactively or retroactively, we will ground our intervention in principles that help us understand the person in relation to themselves, others, and their community. Most effective intervening includes understanding, more than the tool, the person(s) responsible for implementing that approach. If we don't consider the implementers who are applying the intervention, we can easily reinforce a particular behavior and inadvertently cause further damage. Having a theory to ground the people and the tool helps turn prevention from a strategy toward a paradigm.

There are new theories on human behavior springing up each year. Some of these theories are psychological, developmental, and ecological. As confusing as it can be to find a theory that suits one's personal and professional orientation, it's even more confusing to assess if the philosophical constructs are congruent with the needs of the person or system we seek to help.

Gestalt is one of the oldest of the psychological theories, evolving from psychoanalytic theory. The founders of gestalt psychology and theory moved away from analysis for many reasons, mainly due to an interest in phenomenology and present-centered experience. Rather than attaching meaning only to one's past, gestalt theory attempted to understand people as complex systems where perceptions and experiences are key. If we can make meaning of what we take in from the environment, we can better understand who we are and how we act to get our needs met.

Gestalt theory is useful for the study of school violence because it is used both in psychotherapy as well as organizational consulting, which is seldom seen. Because violence is an amalgamation of various levels of small and large systems, we need a lens that fits intra- an interpersonal functioning within the context of these larger systems.

Gestalt theory is best known for an emphasis on the here and now, indicating we are concerned with what we are attending to in this very place and moment, bringing our focus to what is as opposed to what was. We look at the past in the context of the present, trying to discover what is unfinished and how we have been influenced by what was. Violence, even if it's impulsive, is in part an enactment of unfinished business in a person who feels unable to live well in the present moment. Violence is also rooted in a person's inability to take ownership of one's experience, instead projecting blame onto others.

For the bully who is constantly looking for validation or the school shooter who can't reconcile their past and present wounds, these violent students are unable to make contact with others in a way that gets their own needs met. They are likely involved with excessive thinking, ruminating about the past and obsessing about their future. They spend time reflecting on situations and wishing for a different future, giving up power by not living in the moment.

In gestalt theory we are interested in three planes of existence, including the self in relation to the self, the self in relation to others, and the self in relation to the world. This is useful when exploring violence because of the multiple systems and influences that influence the act of aggression. As a person who is inside or outside of the system, we want to recognize that the process of examining our experience/perception in relation to others is even more important than any outcome or conclusion we may reach.

What is figural for potentially catastrophically violent students may be threat, oppression, and retaliation. They tend to see others as prospective persecutors who either injure through action or inaction. The ground for these students may be a combination of grief/loss, grandiose fantasy, and disengagement. The figure and ground interact to create a diffusion of reality and fantasy that is both hopeless and vengeful. With these students there is a tendency toward extremes that helps them escape experience of what's real.

Polarities are the extremes of each continuum in which we observe a phenomenon. Rather than saying, "That boy is weak," we would instead encourage the person making the interpretation to instead consider their subjective experience of this boy along a continuum from passive to aggressive. This boy may not be passive in situations where the observer isn't present, so we aren't able to make a definitive statement that categorizes him. Even if we did, the act of doing so will both color how we treat that child and likely how that child acts in our presence.

Description is considered more important than prescription or interpretation. People are helped to find their own meaning as opposed to taking on the beliefs of others. If we don't judge the child as passive, we can help the child take ownership of their passivity. A child will resist a label or perhaps submit to that label, but in doing so there is no exploration of why she is the way she is. We would much rather a child become curious and, possibly, develop new awareness by paying attention to one's self. A child who is being bullied may recognize his own actions and interactions that help him to be in the victim role, offering him opportunity to create experiments designed to increase his potency.

Helping people take responsibility for their lives is an important step in reducing violence. If we can stop blaming others for what we feel, we build our power toward creating change. Those students who regress to the point of mass violence are demonstrating the ultimate blame toward their community for how they feel. They exact vengeance to regain power, because they know no other way to feel vital again.

We don't want to confuse taking ownership with exculpating a system for their role in creating a milieu for violence. There are multiple systems working simultaneously, each of which will need to assume responsibility for its piece in the puzzle. Just because a young man needs to assume responsibility for his experience of feeling powerless before condemning a school, so too does the school need to look at its role in creating a culture where this bullying can flourish.

The degree of openness for any system will determine the level of ownership for the impact on its constituents. In a very open system, information is expressed freely across boundaries; people know they are safe to explore differences, and curiosity is encouraged. Open systems tend to value awareness of self, others, and the environment. In a more closed system, rules are more rigid, as are structures that inhibit free expression and creativity.

Open systems utilize a feedback loop that continually informs of deviations from the defining purpose; in the case of schools this involves the input of information and the output of learning. The information obtained from this loop helps to make decisions that allow for pivoting toward maintenance of the system's goals. The degree of openness and learning of the system will impact the degree of entropy, or the natural disintegration of the system. In terms of violence generation, entropy will create increasing tension that members of the system experience as a threat, encouraging those within to move toward a more survivalist mentality.

Over time, school systems become more complex, as most evolving systems do. People have different ideas, needs, and methods of accomplishing their goals. Goals are not always agreed upon, but most often it's the mode of operations that is contested. Differentiation is a process of negotiating that helps to refine and redefine the efficiency and effectiveness of operations. The more productive the process of differentiation, the more likely cohesion will result. The more disruptive the process, the greater the likelihood that tensions will rise and hostilities ensue.

The generation of violence is complicated, and this chapter provides an overview of theoretical constructs to understand the various levels of influence. Gestalt theory emphasizes creative investigation as opposed to fitting behavior into a rigid structure. This means there are no programs that get applied to an institution in the hopes of making it less violent. In fact, the idea that we can insert a prevention program into a system without becoming involved with that system in a more intimate way runs the risk of promoting greater polarization within. If we attempt to understand what is figural for the student, we begin a truly transformative process as opposed to what is more commonly known as transitional or incremental change.

QUESTIONS TO CONSIDER

1. What other theories of violence and human behavior am I aware of?
2. If I have an existing violence-prevention program, does the program talk about the paradigm from which the strategies were based?
3. If our school were to embrace a theoretical perspective on violence, how would we go about the process since everybody isn't likely to endorse the same ideas?
4. How might having a theoretical orientation around violence, behavioral management, or even learning impact our school culture? Our daily operations?

TWELVE
Involving Parents

Jay is a seventh-grade social studies teacher in Indiana. One Thursday morning he was taken out of his classroom by a school administrator, who led him to the conference room without saying a word to him. In the room he and another teacher were instructed to listen to a parent without responding. The parent seemed hateful from the moment Jay walked into the room, using harsh language, even expletives to express her anger. "You are lousy teachers and don't deserve your job," said the parent to Jay, as the other teacher escaped through the door crying.

Jay was unfortunately used to this type of reaction as it wasn't the first time he felt verbally assaulted by a parent; however, it was the first time an administrator had witnessed the whole thing without intervening. Jay couldn't decide what was worse, the way he was spoken to by the parent or the fact that the administrator seemed okay with it. Nobody seemed to care that this parent's child had regularly come to class unprepared, refused invitations from the teacher to stay late and get caught up, and was failing class. All the parent seemed concerned with was the student's grade and how it was the teacher's fault.

Scenarios such as this one are taking place all across the country and with greater frequency. Administrators seem afraid to set limits, not wanting parents to complain to their superiors, leaving teachers feeling unsupported. Teachers, not on their own, become conflicted between the instinct for self-protection and their natural instinct to help their student. If the teacher opts for safety, he may withdraw from the child and not extend any extra effort.

This type of scenario occurs when parents aren't clear about how to best support their child, going on the offensive instead of forming a strong working relationship with their child's teacher. Parents sometimes forget they aren't just raising their children to be successful in school, they are preparing them to be well adjusted in life. This means learning how to deal with problems constructively, which will help reduce the potential that children will consider violence as a viable option for upset.

If we want to have schools we can feel proud of, we might consider the home as part of the community that influences the school. Students make up over two-thirds of every school building, so their impact on the culture of each school is enormous. With emerging value sets, strong characters, and growing resiliency, our children have the influence to create inspirational and safe school communities.

Involving parents can take many different forms from developing handbooks to creating parenting classes. The key is creativity so that parents are motivated to participate. Understanding that schools are doing all they can to develop a new paradigm and strongly need the parents to be part of this transformative process is a good beginning. With devoted school employees, outside consultants, or even parents volunteers (Parent-Teacher Association/Organization), the planning can begin to address several areas outlined in this chapter that support nonviolence.

There are broad and specific tasks parents must attend to in order to raise nonviolent children. Our goals for this chapter are to help parents feel empowered to raise nonviolent children while offering meaningful contributions for a healthy school community. Parents who read this book will be doing their homework as part of the collective goal of school improvement.

To return as an educational leader in the world, this country needs to rebuild communities that nurture growth and promote openness. A fertile ground of safety and possibility allows for effective teaching of both basic and advanced skills, critical thinking, facts, formulas, and principles that prepare children for higher learning. Our colleges and universities are sought out by foreign scholars across the globe, and with work our primary and secondary schools can regain this same prestige.

In order to improve our schools as high-quality learning environments, we first need to improve feelings of safety. We need our children to go to school free from the threat of bullying, gangs, and catastrophic violence. If and when tragedy does occur, we need to be prepared to address this as a learning experience to grow from and not a spark plug that ignites copycat violence across the country, perpetual blame, and widespread panic. Fortunately, the very process of preventing violence will also prepare schools who deal with this unfortunate tragedy.

The sturdy foundation from which to accomplish this includes healthy students who internalize the ideal of nonviolence as a crucial element in an evolving society. This value is learned at home and reinforced in school, woven into their curricula from elementary school onward through secondary school. We can instill this lesson at any time in our child's life by quieting the voice that promotes blame and entitlement. For those parents who are already proud of what we have accomplished in this realm, never let your guard down, because there are always new lessons to reinforce these ideals.

For the well-intended but sometimes complacent parent, remember that for every attribute we have promoted, there is a corresponding limitation to be aware of. If we have been exceedingly patient and indulgent, we may have established fewer limits that promote a tolerance for delayed gratification. If we have been on top of everything our children do, leaving little room for them to misbehave without consequences, we have done less to promote freedom. Polarities exist in everything, helping us to appreciate the value of balance and the need for constant adjustments.

Parenting can be described as the ongoing process of deliberate adjustments that, over time, are accomplished with less direction from the outside. We want our children to become self-sufficient and use us as guides who walk alongside them as opposed to too far out front or behind. We should be there to help them rebound from disappointment and learn how they may improve areas of deficit while accepting their own inequities. We want them to take responsibility for their actions and tolerate disappointment, and in doing so we will be preparing them well for a more peaceful life.

The following outlines eight critical areas in greater depth in our consideration of raising nonviolent children.

ALLOW CHILD TO EXPERIENCE FAILURE (STOP ENABLING)

A growing trend in parenting, and perhaps society, is overcorrection toward rewarding to prevent disappointment for the intent of self-esteem preservation. The overcorrection is generated by a strong sense of protectiveness out of fear our children will feel poorly about themselves. This is occurring both at home with fearful parents and in the schools with educators who worry about parental reactions. In schools we sometimes offer awards for children regardless of whether they are deserved to prevent kids from feeling like they didn't succeed. At home, parents rush to the rescue of their children to help them avert feelings of hurt or sadness, especially in middle- and upper-class communities.

An increasing number of parents seem to have a difficult time allowing their children to fail. At first glance this may seem like an obvious job for a parent, to help their child find success and avoid failure, but in fact it's only half the job. The other half is helping children learn how to deal with disappointment, which means we have to allow for them to not succeed in spite of their best efforts. We are raising a generation of children who don't know what it means to fail and aren't prepared mentally or emotionally to deal with the feelings arising from not getting what they want.

"Failure," of course, is a provocative term, cautioning us to pay more attention to effort over outcome. If our child tries hard, is well intended, and doesn't achieve the desired outcome, the success is their effort. Thus we want to avoid the trap of putting our energy into changing the outcome. If we focus on what they did well, we can build them up while preparing them for the likelihood that not everything goes our way in life.

The term "helicopter parents" was initially used to describe parents who hover over their children, pointing out potential dangers that may thwart achievement. The term also describes parents who are overly controlling and interfere with the natural social and academic processes of their kids in school. While helicopter parents may believe they are doing right by their children, they are in fact preventing them from learning how to cope when something doesn't go their way.

Teachers become frustrated by these parents because they can quickly undermine a teacher's authority while lessening accountability on the part of the student. It may come in the form of fighting with a teacher for a higher grade, doing a child's homework for him, or calling another parent to address a social conflict without allowing their child to have a chance to resolve it herself.

This is the case for a suburban Pennsylvania parent whose child did not make safety patrol, a highly coveted honor for the academic and social stars of the elementary school. The parent complained relentlessly to the principal and superintendent, going so far as to block an outing this group took at year's end. She seemed to view the power struggle as something very personal, not caring that she was impacting all the other children who were looking forward to celebrating their hard work.

The superintendent eventually gave in to this parent, as many administrators do when the conflict may generate political problems. The legal and public relations nightmare loomed larger for this particular principal, and the parent eventually got her way. The message sent to the rest of the school community is that if you complain loud enough, you will get your way.

If this message makes its way to the students, the school may face behavioral problems from kids constantly testing limits. Some students may become passively obstinate to get their way, while others may become more forceful like the parent described above. The danger is students learning to manipulate the system instead of learning to navigate their way through it using empathy and negotiation. The long-term result of this issue on a larger scale is a generation of children who are not learning frustration tolerance. Low capacity for distress is a key component of students who commit catastrophic violence.

Tolerating distress is already being diminished by the immediate gratification that comes in this new era of technology. Kids learn to get their needs met almost instantaneously as information is readily available with a few clicks as well as video games that deprive young people of the work that goes into social engagement. It may not seem like much, but the negotiation that goes on in setting up a whiffle ball game is partly responsible for conflict-resolution skills that we have described in the section on constructive differencing.

When kids who get what they want when they want it also have parents who intervene prematurely, the results are problematic. Under these conditions we produce young adults who do not learn to be accountable, have a deficit of problem-solving skills, and lack the emotional maturity to cope with distress, which makes them more likely to be reckless and use poor judgment. These are two of the elements that produce children who resort to extreme measures of self-protection when they feel threatened or are under duress.

If instead of rescuing, hovering, and intervening prematurely, we can help our children cope with their unease and learn more constructive ways of handling problems and managing conflict. The first and most important piece, although well woven into the others, is a greater tolerance for distress. If kids can stay in discomfort longer, they will have a greater range of choices to deal with situations. This does not mean suffering. Holding our hand over a candle to better tolerate pain is foolish and dangerous. Instead, we want our children to endure discomfort that we would expect is reasonable for their age.

In this era of video games and other technologies, children are conditioned by immediate gratification. If we want it, we can have it with lightning speed, such as looking something up on the Internet or shopping for something online. They want to hear a song, they download it from an Internet vendor. Instead of organizing kids on their block to play football, they go online and join an existing virtual game with others.

For better or for worse, this is the nature of our culture that children are growing up in, and this requires making adjustments on the part of parents. If our children don't learn to delay gratification or endure the stress of not having their needs met right away, they will become entitled and fragile. This will make them targets for their peers who prey upon perceived weakness. They may become the subject of bullying, which they handle less well than the everyday stressors.

IMPROVE CAPACITY FOR DISTRESS

How parents can help their children improve their capacity for distress is the single most underappreciated task of parenthood. The simple answer is allowing them to fail while teaching them the tools to cope with their disappointment. If your child is embarrassed at getting a low grade on a project, help her to feel understood and then strategize about what she can do differently next time. This doesn't mean we ought to abandon children when help is needed to succeed; this is about after the fact when their best wasn't good enough.

Teach ownership for their role in the outcome of everything they are involved with, and you will raise likable kids, with high integrity, who push themselves toward high achievement. Do the opposite—raise somebody who blames others—and you will find your child becomes whiney and bitter. Allowing a child to feel the natural disappointment or rejection from not attaining his objectives on a particular task gives him a chance to grieve. Once he grieves, he can begin strategizing by learning from his actions and planning for his next goal.

If a child takes responsibility for why she didn't achieve her desired outcome and doesn't blame others, she will ultimately feel more powerful. Helping children to focus on their effort, creativity, and initiative will help them feel value. If a child truly puts in his best effort, he will feel pride. Even if you believe the teacher, for instance, was unfair in her grading, still encourage your child to examine his responsibility and never minimize his role. Doing so will disempower a child, even if it feels like empowering in the moment.

Understanding how your child feels as opposed to looking at outcomes is a simple yet highly underrated parenting role. For most parents, it does not feel like doing enough to simply listen and acknowledge feelings. Contrary to our instinct to do more, being empathic is the single most powerful and effective tool in the parental repertoire. Being there to support and console, not to blame or fix, can help children bounce back quicker from letdowns. For those parents who simply must do more, you can let your child know that you believe in her, point out other times she has achieved desired results, and encourage her through pride at her resiliency.

"I know you feel discouraged because your coach didn't put you in the game. I was sad too at not getting to see you play. I'm very proud of you for cheering on your teammates and sticking with it, even though it's not as fun for you right now." In this example, the parent isn't intervening or giving advice, simply staying with their child's feeling, sharing feelings of his own, and encouraging stick-to-it-iveness. If the situation were to continue, there are other options, but only after you have allowed for the child to handle it herself.

Another way of promoting increased frustration tolerance is to help children imagine what they went through and how they would approach it again given another opportunity. This is different from regret and rumination, which can help people stay stuck. This reflection is intended to empower by reviewing one's own actions and creating strategies to apply for the future.

In the case of the student who sat on the bench and watched the game, there wasn't much that could have been done, and so this would not be a helpful strategy. In this instance, a child can anticipate what she might do if she is given the opportunity. She can also look at how to serve her team in other ways. Can she learn something from watching her teammates? Can she give support to her friends who are playing? Can she inject some humor into the game to keep people relaxed? In theater, children are taught there are no small parts, just small actors.

When action is called for, a rule of thumb is to have your child address the person directly whenever possible. When somebody else is involved, such as a teacher, we want to help children learn how to be their own advocates. As soon as parent comes to a child's rescue, two things are likely to happen. The adult is going to become defensive, and the child is going to become fearful of the outcome. Using good common sense and judgment will tell you when sending your child in to negotiate for himself is indicated, as there are often times it can be unproductive and even aggravate the situation for the child to do it alone.

When a situation allows for a child to stand up for himself, which is nearly always the case when it comes to another child who is not physically overpowering or endangering him, it's important for be prepared with an arsenal of peaceful negotiation skills. Resolving differences amicably is the single most important skill a child will learn that determines his success socially. Since differences are a routine part of every day, it's imperative a child knows how to work toward compromise and differentiation without sacrificing his integrity.

If your child comes home and complains about being picked on, your first action isn't to call the school and set up a meeting with the principal. Unless it's an extreme circumstance in which serious threats or harm have befallen your child, you want your child thinking through her options and feeling capable not powerless. She may decide telling an adult is the best course of action, and she can be coached on how to do this respectfully and assertively. It's not always easy to distinguish between situations requiring your involvement, so let your child be the guide. Children will often know when something is within their volition to address if they haven't been rescued every step of the way.

If you are a parent who didn't bring your newborn in public for the first six months of life, made everyone wash their hands before handling the baby, removed every obstacle in the room, and caught your child each time before falling, you may have already created an expectation that he will be rescued early and often. Attend to your own fears, and try not to allow them to dictate your actions; otherwise you will have a child who seeks out help before attempting to intervene on her own behalf.

TEACH PROBLEM SOLVING

Teaching problem solving is one of the more challenging tasks a parent has because it involves several components, such as critical thinking, awareness of self in relation to others, empathy, compromise, creativity, and an understanding of developmental norms. A child who is six, for instance, is going to find answers to problems that may seem unsophisticated but are based on the type of thinking associated with that age.

To keep it as simple as possible, we want to encourage the children to come up with as many possible strategies as they can. Help them anticipate the potential benefits and consequences of each to promote discrimination skills. Role playing can be a way to help children see unexpected outcomes of their approach.

Looking ahead also teaches children to be more thoughtful and less impulsive. Through dialogue, provide encouragement for creativity and try to refrain from judging their ideas. If they can determine which of their ideas is the most constructive they will feel more proud of themselves and be least likely to blame you as the parent if they aren't successful.

If we encourage our child to ask others how they deal with similar situations, he will be helped to brainstorm better for himself. Ultimately, he will need to make a decision that fits for him on both a cognitive level and a gut level. If he is choosing between solutions that don't have clearly preferred upsides, he may look to which choices have the fewest risks. This of course depends on his risk-tolerance level, which as a parent you want to illuminate. If he is prepared for worst-case scenarios, he is prepared for that particular choice.

Oftentimes problem solving can be done alongside another person. Bringing others into the problem-solving process, especially if they are involved in the problem, can serve as the solution itself. Even if agreement isn't reached, the act of working together with another person can diffuse tensions. If a child has empathy for the other person and values what others believe, she will find support more available. If she doesn't consider others' feelings and is dismissive of new ideas, she may struggle.

HOLD ACCOUNTABLE

Holding your child accountable is another important objective for parents in raising violence-free children. Everybody makes mistakes, and children are more apt to do so than adults. Childhood is a continuous process of experimentation and risk taking, which more often than not results in poor choices. Judgment is based on their stage of moral development, typically leading kids to overestimate their capabilities and act in a self-serving manner. In the early teen years, they still lack foresight, neglect to anticipate the consequences of their actions, and are impulsive and driven by base instincts. Only when they are taught ownership of their behavior do they mature in these areas.

When a child does something regrettable, we want to encourage honesty first in accurately reporting her role of the situation. A child's first instinct is often to lie, omit, minimize, and cover up because she doesn't want to get into trouble, often fearing her parents' reaction and consequences in general. Kids don't want to be ostracized or feel their parents' disappointment, so they give us a revisionist version of events.

If we want to encourage kids to be accurate reporters of events, we want to remind them of this early in the reporting process but also pay attention to our verbal and nonverbal responses. If we seem judgmental from the onset, they will get this vibe and deviate from the truth. Reinforcing the idea that their parents will be pleased with them for owning their actions in spite of what they have done is a helpful way to encourage taking responsibility.

If a child returns home from school to report that his teacher treated him unfairly, we want to avoid being prematurely critical and questioning, but neither do we want to take up arms in his defense as described earlier. Contrary to common belief, our job is *not* to evaluate the situation after gathering all the data. We do this only when our child is in over his head and needs our intervention.

In situations where our child seems harmed and in need of our active support, our job is still to first listen to how she shares what has taken place, paying close attention to a few things. Is she sharing information as well as her feelings? Helping children to process their feelings can often negate the need to take further action. Is she blaming or taking ownership for her piece, no matter how small? Even if she is speculating about what her contribution was, this is helpful.

The recent suicide of Rebecca Sedwick in response to what appears to have been relentless bullying and cyberbullying brings this question of parental responsibility into the spotlight. In spite of a message appearing on the Facebook page of one of the alleged perpetrators, which reads "Yes, I know I bullied REBECCA and she killed herself, but IDGAF," the girl's parents deny their daughter had any involvement. If the parents did in fact know and didn't intervene, what level of accountability will they be held to?

If we don't learn to hold our children accountable for their actions, we will send a message that they are beyond reproach. The children in these families will test limits more, be dishonest to cover up their mistakes, and intrude on the boundaries of others without regret or remorse. If we don't hold our children accountable and send the message that they can do no wrong, condoning them, making excuses, blaming others, and so on, we will raise children who are capable of traumatic bullying.

A parent's job goes beyond teaching children to take ownership to teaching them to stand up to others whom they see as being bullies. Becoming an upstander, somebody who takes action when they see somebody being unfairly treated, is part of our responsibility as a citizen of the school and beyond, for creating a nonviolent community.

MODELING NONVIOLENCE

Modeling nonviolence is an obvious but vital part of the equation, because children learn more from what you do than what you say. If you spank a child for hitting his sibling, you are sending a confusingly mixed message that often leads children to take in the punishment more than their own behavior. If you yell obscenities at a driver who cut you off, threaten a child with punishment, or become physical with your spouse, you are teaching your children how to deal with conflict in the most unhealthy of ways.

Understanding how we internalized messages around anger and aggression from our own upbringing can be a good beginning. Whether we are on the passive or aggressive side of the continuum, we have undoubtedly learned and passed along both subtle and overt messages about violence, which we want to address outwardly. Talking with our children at the dinner table is a good way to assess what their views are and how we as parents have influenced them in their particular direction. Bringing up incidents that take place in society, such as vigilantism, and gauging their opinion will tell you where growth may be needed. If they believe that somebody who has done harm to another deserves corporal punishment, we might ask ourselves how this view impacts their own approach to problem solving with peers.

When it comes to navigating the differences we have with our children's teachers, we are being watched closely by our kids to see how we respond, especially when we become frustrated. Remember that it's not enough to vigorously advocate for our child; we must also attend to the larger community and the way in which our actions help to shape the school culture. Even if we are angry with the sometimes questionable judgments of adults in charge of caring for and teaching our children, we want to walk away from the conflict in a way that helps us feel better about the situation but also ourselves. If our children could have watched us handle the situation, consider whether or not they would be proud.

As a parent, we may not realize the importance of reflecting upon how we negotiate differences in order to get our needs met. Do we protect ourselves through threat or intimidation? Do others feel oppressed after interacting with us? Do our children ever listen out of fear not of punishment but retribution? Even if we believe we are justified in how we deal with others, we must remain mindful that our children are watching our every move, learning more from what we do than what we say. Consequently, being on the other side of the continuum—overly passive—can also teach our children to accept mistreatment.

Interviews with teachers from across the country have suggested a rise in parent bullish behavior. Teachers are experiencing demanding parents who yell, threaten, and persist to a level of harassment when trying to get their way. When educators experience a parent's anger or the threat of repercussion, such as rallying the other parents to damage the educator's reputation or going to the higher-ups in the district to disempower the educator, the result may be greater apathy and detachment. Teachers need to be treated as allies and not adversaries, even when there is disagreement, partly to demonstrate to our kids that working cooperatively serves our own interest and the greater good.

It isn't fair to intimate that kids who become bullies at school are bullied by parents at home. It's too broad a generalization to assume such a direct correlation, and research hasn't been conclusive. It is fair to estimate that kids who are being bullies at school have not learned or don't feel compelled to behave in a nonviolent manner, so we need to ask ourselves if we are doing enough proactively.

The National School Safety Center, a leading authority in this area, found through cooperative research with the Centers for Disease Control that about 80 percent of bullies were first themselves victims of bullies in the form of parents, peers, siblings, or others.[1] Many victims evolve into perpetrators as a reaction to their own experiences with ridicule, physical punishment, torment, and abuse. Thus it is important to recognize how many children progress along a continuum toward violence if that has been a consistent part of their upbringing.

SUPPORT THE LEARNING PROCESS

There has been a significant shift in the role of parents in education. Whereas teachers were once revered and seldom questioned, leaving parents to hold their children entirely responsible for their learning successes and failures, we now view education vastly differently. Through the advent of legislative acts, parent–teacher organizations, and other political action, we have seen a shift toward a different polarity.

Michael Hickley wrote a chapter called "Parents, Power, and the Politics of School Reform" (from the book *Power, Politics, and Ethics in School Districts*) that sums up this change well. "Parent representatives' primary concerns all too often were for their own children (perhaps understandably), and the result was a fragmented and at times self-serving perspective that lost sight of the forest for the sake of the (family) tree."[2]

If parents intercede on behalf of their child, they will be best served by asking both what is in the best interest of the child and the school as a whole. Without doing so, changes may be accomplished but at the expense of the system. In the instance we saw earlier, a guidance counselor in a suburban school used to be responsible for the child safety patrol, a group of exemplary students selected by their teachers to serve as role models and supports for their peers. One parent, using her power as head of the PTO, persistently lobbied for her child to be placed on the team despite the fact that there were nominations by the teachers. While protests to administrators in the school district and persistent pressure on the counselor ultimately resulted in her getting her way, she didn't consider the ultimate cost for the system.

Not only did the school counselor retire from his position as adult supervisor for this group, the entire safety patrol ultimately disbanded. The kids on the team never got to go on their field trip to celebrate their involvement, and disappointment spread among the students and parents. The ripple effect from this type of situation can extend far from the event itself, leaving a wake of damage extending well beyond the incident.

A parent's primary job when it comes to education is to support the learning process. Parents oversee their children's education by ensuring there is good communication with the teacher, providing rewards and consequences to keep their children motivated, and helping kids to deal with the emotional strain of increasing challenges. Parenting is like driving a speedboat in the ocean, with constant waves jostling the small boat. If we try to outrun the wave, we will be imbalanced and potentially capsized. If we head directly into the wave, we will feel the bump but not risk being capsized.

Parents need to support the work being done in the school and the educators who are doing it. A reason most of us don't teach our children is because we aren't objective. Parents don't typically possess the patience or impartiality to remain neutral, whether it's regarding our children's grades or a dispute they are having with another student. Like teaching a child to swim, we might be horrified to see our child swallow water. If the child becomes too afraid to continue, we might not push, while a certified instructor knows that sparking a child's natural instinct to stay afloat is what's needed to promote learning.

Parents can support school transformation through lending their time, energy, and insight into the growth process. The outside perspective of parents can help those who are within the school gain a greater appreciation of what may not be seen, such as the struggle a child has to work independently with homework. As long as this information is communicated in a way that isn't blaming or judgmental, educators will be receptive to the input. Clever educators will value the data as useful to their own learning process and do their best to keep reciprocal feedback loops in place.

Parents will be helped in this endeavor by asking themselves whether their advocacy is in support of learning or grades. Learning is the process that is vital to developing adaptive students who can function independently when school is over, while grades are the outcomes we tend to overemphasize due to college admissions requirements. Thus we can address apparent inequity but do so with the awareness that winning a skirmish can be defeating for everybody in the long run.

Parents who view themselves as part of the school community will address issues in the spirit of the system as opposed to being the lone representative for their child. Keep in mind that school transformation involves constructive exploration of differences that expand our knowledge base and open our eyes wider to possibilities.

PROMOTE EMPATHY

Young adults who learn to put themselves in the shoes of others will have greater success in life. Empathy allows for better negotiation skills, deeper friendships, greater intimacy in romantic relationships, better predication of others and events, increased self-awareness through learning from others, and a greater sense of well-being from caring and helping others. Kids who learn to be empathic will be less likely to perpetrate or be the recipient of intentional violence.

School-aged children who understand the needs, feelings, and actions of others will not be as likely to take things personally; plus they will lend helpful support to those in distress. As an asset, they may be less likely targeted by others because their value quotient has gone up. Similarly, kids who are empathic will be less threated by others, more self-assured, and less likely to pick on somebody less powerful or fortunate than themselves. Instead, they will be sensitive to differences and stand up for those who need help.

The upstander movement is a way of promoting empathy in schools, acting on children's compassion and sense of justice to address mistreatment of others. Parents can help this movement by doing their part to teach empathy at home, where children learn that it's not enough to do the right thing but that we also need to help our community toward the same end. If your child reported he had a good day, ask him if he witnessed anybody else struggling academically or socially. Encourage him to get involved and offer his help, even if it means taking a risk without seriously jeopardizing his safety.

Helping our children to look at events through the eyes of others including teachers, peers, and even bullies can help them determine how they may intercede when action is needed. Understanding what it's like to be bullied, for instance, will provide motivation to overcome the fear of standing up to injustice, because they won't feel comfortable knowing somebody is suffering and they did nothing about it. Empathy will ignite a child's natural sense of what is right versus wrong to help her do what is needed and allow her to feel peace of mind. Empathy will help children to address all the difficult situations and conflicts they are part of by appreciating that right or wrong exists far less frequently than young people imagine.

COMMUNICATION BETWEEN HOME AND SCHOOL

A gap often exists between parents and teachers, allowing children to fall through the cracks. Several reasons exist for this gap, most often attributed to the privacy families maintain about their lives. Understandably, parents don't want their personal lives to be a matter of public record, interfering with their social and academic goals. Thus, they withhold sometimes important information that would be helpful in supporting the learning process and on occasion vital data that could prevent the evolution of catastrophic violence.

Helping parents to feel safe in sharing personal information is the goal and the first step in building communication with parents. If you aren't aware of the existing trust levels, it can be helpful to conduct both formal and informal polls to gather this information. If it is determined that trust isn't high enough to support meaningful and consistent dialogue with parents and teachers, work needs to be done to build this trust. Keep in mind that trust can vary widely according to the specific facets of trust being measured.

By nature of developing a unified paradigm of violence prevention that parents will be involved in creating, opportunities for building or restoring trust will be generated. As long as parents don't feel blamed by schools for raising violent kids, they may be more receptive to being part of the team. Parents may find it easier to reach out to other parents in instances where teachers won't be successful.

Let parents know that the goals for this new approach are mutually beneficial but also mutually dependent. Parents can't help their students without knowing what's going on in their schools, and schools can't help without understanding the dynamics of a student's home life. This contingency will allow for movement away from a punitive-based system that evokes shame and fear to a more nurturing and awareness-driven model that looks at the underlying motives for behavior.

If parents are helped to appreciate a school's intent to look deeper than a child's actions, understanding what needs aren't being met, and how this shows up in terms of relational, social, academic, and other observable behaviors, they will be more likely to cooperate. If parents recognize the value in building consistency between home and school, so that students know they are being held accountable without one side being played against the other, motivation will also increase. Consistency of rewards and consequences can significantly improve a child's behavior, but even if differences exist between the different worlds, children will adapt. Communication between home and school will ultimately help both sides appreciate what works best, learning from each other throughout the school year.

Once the barriers of trust have been navigated, the school should set their intention to enhance their understanding of students. Most specifically we want to target changes in behavior, attitude, emotionality, socializing, academics, and other areas that signal the potential decline of a student's psychological health. Building this early-warning detection system can help schools ascertain the nature of these changes, deciding where intervention efforts are needed. Schools that do this effectively will stop problems before they blossom into nightmarish outcomes.

Imagine a situation in which a parent of a student notified the teacher that the parents are moving in the direction of divorce. The teacher now matches this information with the student's recent agitation in class and, after checking this out with other faculty, discovers social isolation as well. The two groups of caregivers and educators work together to identify a child in distress.

QUESTIONS TO CONSIDER

1. How would I assess our overall relationship with parents in the school?
2. How involved do we encourage parents to be in both classroom learning and school operations? How much do we protect ourselves against the intrusion of parents?
3. If we view parents as an underutilized resource for the improvement of school culture and the reduction of violence potential, how might we begin to enlist their help?
4. How can we help improve communication with parents so that we are alerted to the significant life changes and risk factors that correlate with student aggression?
5. How do we help raise awareness of parents for the warning signs of violence and work to improve parenting skills and improved family functioning without seeming intrusive?

NOTES

1. "Bullying Statistics," http://www.fbi.gov/stats-services/publications/law-enforcement-bulletin/may_2011/school_violence.
2. Michael Hickley and Francis M. Duffy, *Power, Politics, and Ethics in School Districts: Dynamic Leadership for Systematic Change* (Lanham, MD: Rowman and Littlefield Education, 2006).

THIRTEEN
Using Technology Safely

Schools generally have a faculty member responsible for technology, although in some smaller schools this may be handled inside each classroom. This is a tremendous responsibility because the person is responsible not only for educating students on the use of technology but also the safe use of this vehicle. Similar to driver's education, we don't just want to teach the mechanics of driving but the awesome responsibility that comes with operating a potentially lethal weapon.

Those responsible for technology must not only be aware of what they are promoting in the school but what students have access to in their everyday lives. This may seem to fall outside the scope of responsibility for educators, but if it's not assumed under the umbrella of education, the risk has now elevated—leaving it up to parents to monitor and supervise their children. If any school feels comfortable doing this they are setting themselves up for disaster.

Technology may include social networking sites, mobile phone applications, or other electronic equipment that allows for virtual interaction with others. Educators want to stay ahead of the curve by knowing what trends are current and upcoming. Reading a technology blog or magazine is a simple way to accomplish this.

Schools have new technology available to them every day. Some embrace this medium as a platform for learning and guide children in using this tool responsibly while others are fearful and limit exposure. The more conservative schools that restrict access and use of high-tech devices do so because they view this medium as a potential disruption to education or a risk to student privacy.

In fairness to many school officials who are spending their days putting out fires started during and often times after school hours, technology may be hazardous. School officials have a difficult enough time preventing bullying and social problems on school property, and now we are asking them to deal with issues arising at home. Add to the complexity of this task a lack of reliable information and anonymity that obscures ascertaining reliable data, and we have put schools in a very difficult situation. When an educator feels powerless, more extreme methods of intervening may follow.

If educators can refrain from blaming parents and parents can in turn join the school in constructive problem solving, the collaborative effort will yield better results. Some useful guidelines for schools in helping students use technology safer may include the following:

- Regular meetings between parents and educators are needed to keep everybody in the loop about what issues and technologies are trending.
- Issues that arise between students springing forth from social media need to be addressed early.
- Class time needs to be spent, either by a trained teacher or an outside consultant, on the safe use of social media, texting, and other technologies.
- Consequences for infractions need to be logical and related, not punitive.

When problems do arise, we might shift our intention to opportunity driven as opposed to distraction driven. There is a lesson inherent in nearly every infraction. If we can remember this, we won't go straight for behavioral modification but seek to uncover the underlying issues and potential growth opportunities from all future unfortunate or even tragic events.

If we appreciate the idea that every misbehavior is a message to the community that somebody is hurting, we may find greater patience in facilitating problem solving. Kids don't typically harass, demean, or belittle others simply because they are evil. Most times children don't recognize what is driving their own behavior and need a responsible adult to help them look inward.

Imagine if we catch students early in their acting out, helping them to identify needs that aren't being met, identifying ways to help them cope more effectively. Doing so may prevent them from becoming perpetrators, which is more likely if on top of not having needs met they face strictly punitive responses without feeling cared for. Perpetrators of violence are generally young people who don't believe any option other than aggression will work, making it necessary to teach them viable options. These lessons need to be deeply ingrained, otherwise the freedoms that come with Internet use will be abused. Establishing parameters of safe Internet use and responsible citizenship are messages students need to hear on a consistent basis.

Simple strategies to be considered by school districts, which can be sponsored by Parent-Teacher Associations, community programs, business partnerships, private practitioners, and so on at minimal or no cost to the school include:

- Parenting classes offered through the school or coordinated by the school on managing social media and dealing constructively with differences
- Encouraging free expression, constructive posting, and experimentation with entrepreneurship
- Differentiating disagreeing from disregarding/diminishing
- Recognizing sexual maturation and the risk taking that accompanies this stage of development
- Discussing safe sites and Internet caution
- Setting boundaries about what gets posted, including pictures and stories, and
- Explaining how to safely use online journaling for anonymity.

The Internet is a tool that, like any tool, requires experience, maturity, limits, and supervision. We wouldn't allow a seven-year-old to operate a power drill, so why would we allow him to surf the Internet by himself?

Parents who aren't familiar with the Internet nearly to the same degree as their children are may find it difficult to monitor usage; however, like anything else our children do in school, we must educate ourselves to be helpful. Keeping the computer in a public part of the house to decrease the temptation to misuse the Internet is a must for homes with middle-school children. Privacy and filters can be placed on accounts as well so that parents know what their children are doing while adding an extra layer of protection.

Children are going to continue their socializing through texts, social media, and chatting but with a greater sense of anonymity, which breeds a false sense of confidence. Freedom to say and do without the natural filters that exist when we are face to face promotes greater risk taking fueled by impulsivity and poor judgment. Young girls are prime examples, having their reputations permanently scarred by sending naked pictures. Others are damaged by rumors and innuendo, fights promoted by hearsay, and private experiences being broadcast into the public with no way to rescind the act.

If we don't actively and routinely educate students on how to use technology safely, it is more likely they will be damaged in a way that can be difficult to recover from. Even if they are the victims of others' poor judgment and didn't do anything to put themselves in a precarious position, proactive education can help them know how to handle these events with minimal distress. It's similar to taking a defensive driving class that prepares a person for the less predictable actions of others.

Children feel safe when they are held accountable, and the school needs to model this if they have any hope of reinforcing this lesson. An educator who tells students one thing and does another may actually increase the likelihood children will behave inappropriately because they believe they can get away with it and use their adult role model as an excuse.

Accountability also serves the purpose of building integrity into a school climate, because people aren't afraid to look at themselves and learn. If people take ownership of their work, then they are teaching a valuable lesson to students not to project blame outwardly. If students don't blame others for their feelings, they will less likely resort to catastrophic acts of violence, which are in essence punishments to their community for the perceived slights they have endured. Taking ownership starts with the upper level of administration and filters all the way down to the students. Consider the following letter from a school principal, written to parents following several concerning incidents at the school.

> *Dear School Parents,*
>
> *As we all know, the age of technology is fully upon us and changing daily. It seems that children are immersed as early as two years of age, and schools nationwide are challenged to balance students' on-screen time with the socialization and interpersonal communication skills (tone of voice, presence, facial expression, articulation, etc.) they need to be good citizens. HFS is no exception.*
>
> *In the world of social media, e.g., Facebook and Instagram, teachers work tirelessly to convey to students the pitfalls of posting private information in a public forum. Recently, we have had instances of younger children, who apparently have their own accounts, posting derogatory pictures and text paramount to cyberbullying. In most cases, these postings happen at home. The targeted students then come to school feeling hurt and angry, the result of which is an escalation that completely derails learning. To be sure, the negative aspects of social media are not specific to HFS. This issue is one of the most widely addressed at Heads' gatherings and education seminars nationwide.*
>
> *The reality is that kids do not have a magic switch that they can turn off to leave their emotions at the door. They enter school feeling embarrassed, hurt, angry, and anxious about facing their peers. To put it succinctly, these issues that originate outside of school impede learning inside of our walls; upset students shut down academically, and teachers are devoting valuable class time dealing with the aftermath and redirecting students to the task at hand. When they happen in school, it is because students have violated the terms of the Appropriate Technology Acceptable Use Agreement, which they signed in the beginning of the year, not to mention the school rule that they relinquish their phones to their homeroom teacher in the morning and retrieve them at dismissal time!*
>
> *In truth, children, even though middle school, have not fully developed the emotional maturity to process the dangers of misuse, with all of their ramifica-*

tions. Kids live in the moment, not in the realm of cause and effect. In order to promote safety and student responsibility, we need your help.

First, we ask that any necessary contact between students and parents during the school day happen through the front office, not via cell phone, for clear communication and child safety. In terms of establishing controls for your children, we encourage you to open joint accounts, or at the very least, keep current on your children's (changing) passwords; insist on daily review of ALL of their messages and Facebook pages; check the history to be aware of new accounts they try to open without your knowledge (that's a biggie!); communicate with them regularly; and monitor not only outgoing messages but incoming messages as well. These practices will not only help prevent cyberbullying but will also protect THEM from media predators who would seek to harm them.

Acknowledge to them that owning these tools is not a right; it's a privilege. As long as you are paying the bills, you own the rights to their stuff, especially as it is in their best interest. One of our goals is to make all children feel safe, and we are determined to be proactive and consider changes to our current policy for next year. Please feel free to call, ask questions, or even offer strategies that you have found helpful and effective. We welcome your insights!

Pay attention to your first reaction after reading this letter. Ask yourself how your role as an educator, administrator, parent, and so on may influence the reaction you are having. Imagine what type of climate might be found in this school, as measured by the open and closed continuum. How about the leadership and the influence this principal may have on the faculty? Even imagine how the parents feel in this school around the way in which communication conveys messages about the expectations from the principal.

The parent who shared this document felt blamed and abandoned by the school, leaving little hope that the administrator was interested in looking at the school's role in students' treatment of each other. Telling the parents that the issues originated at home may have been the case, but it meant that the school could abdicate responsibility and insist parents do a better job in managing their children. Even if it were the case that parents were not doing a good job of supervising their children's Internet use, it's not likely they would feel more motivated after reading this letter.

This could have been an opportunity to create unity between the school and family subsystems, making better contact by framing the issue as a joint problem to be solved by everybody involved. Parents may not feel well equipped to help their children become more responsible Internet users, and schools don't necessarily believe it's their place or have the time to devote to this issue. With each side waiting for the other to fix the issue, the problem becomes more entrenched with wider reaching repercussion.

QUESTIONS TO CONSIDER

1. Who in the school is responsible for educating students around the hazards of technology and the responsible use of this medium? What is their training, and what percentage of their time is dedicated to this issue?
2. How much time does the technology coordinator—or if none exists, each teacher—spend becoming familiar with the advent of new social-networking sites, mobile applications, and other advances in technology that children use? How aware are you of the risk factors associated with them?
3. What is the school's policy around cyberbullying, and how well does that policy seem to be working?
4. What is the school's relationship with law enforcement to handle allegations or suspected misconduct around cyberbullying?

FOURTEEN
Harnessing Social Media

With the rise in popularity of social media, our challenge to promote safety and responsibility is increasingly complex. Social media has become the new medium for social norming. Relationships start and end on social media and involve nearly every aspect of a person's life. We learn how to gain popularity and influence others through our digital posts with wide reach for our words and images. This new wave of openness involves sharing nearly every aspect of our lives with friends and family who are both close and distant on the intimacy continuum.

Other distinct aspects of social media's impact on society include,

- Gaining immediate feedback from "likes," retweets, comments, and ratings
- Using blogs such as Tumblr that serve as online diaries
- A sharp decline in privacy that quickly escalates conflicts into mass feuds and
- The emergence of online bullying, which can devastate a life in hours.

Putting derogatory or defaming remarks on somebody's Facebook page can devastate a reputation in a matter of minutes. One young girl who made the unfortunate mistake of sharing an intimate photo with a friend learned that within days of having a falling out with that person, their private image was used to humiliate her publically.

Another young woman confronted a friend who was using drugs and having unprotected sex at an early age, having this one-time friend turn on her viciously. Rumors were spread about her on Twitter, and within days the girl who was trying to help had her reputation decimated by lies.

There are hundreds if not thousands of these incidents occurring every day. There is little accountability for what kids do online, giving them free reign to behave outrageously. Police are inundated with investigations into alleged bullying, and schools are at a loss as to how to protect kids during nonschool hours and debate whether it's even their responsibility to do so. We have limited data to indicate definitive numbers of cyberbullying and other behaviors that fall into the broader category of harmful manipulation by use of social media, but we do know the danger is high.

In spite of the dangers, schools try to harness social-media technology as leverage for stimulating education. Schools exercise varying degrees of caution, some restricting all access to sites that aren't academic in nature, while other teachers are creating lesson plans around these familiar mediums. Schools are right to be confused because we are still in our infancy in terms of learning how to utilize these resources without abuses.

There are advantages to social media that when capitalized can neutralize and even outweigh the significant risks described above. They include:

- Advanced activism potential
- Networking well outside our geographic area
- Greater diversity of data, opinions, ideas, beliefs, and strategies, and
- The opportunity to express oneself and gain immediate feedback.

A NEW LEARNING SITE FOR STUDENTS: UFEUD.COM

It is not the presence of conflict that is to be feared but, rather, its destructive management. Attempts to deny, suppress, repress, and ignore conflicts may, in fact, be a major contributor to the occurrence of violence in schools. Given the many positive outcomes of conflict, schools need to teach students how to manage conflicts constructively.[1]

A contemporary online tool to promote constructive differencing is long overdue. A tool to promote awareness so that conflicts can be explored in a way that helps participants learn about themselves, the issue, and each other is what can ultimately help schools reduce the likelihood of a conflict turning violent.

As our need to engage students becomes more challenging and their ability to problem solve and think critically is deteriorating, it's of the utmost importance that we provide a forum for learning that fits the needs and maintains the interests of our students, whose attention spans are not nearly as long as they once were.

According to Rabbi Yanklowitz,

> Many teachers have observed that students sitting in classrooms today are bored by the frontal authoritarian model of learning.... A curriculum in which they are active participants and engaged in democratic, and cognitively challenging for students works better. In the frontal model, teachers provide the questions and answers. In the argument model, the students provide the questions and the answers while the teachers provide the structure, the facilitation, and the guidance. Students gain the necessary skills to be critical thinkers in a complex society with many different agendas, facts, and perspectives.[2]

In the earlier chapter on constructive differencing, an argument was made for the importance of exploring conflict. It should be reinforced that there are also destructive types of conflict that lead to fractures in relationships. Without proper oversight and an environment that relishes the exploration of differences, conflict can easily devolve to a point where aggression sets in.

To help differentiate constructive from deconstructive conflict we can look to the earlier work of Morton Deutsch[3] as well as that of David Johnson and Roger Johnson.[4] These researchers discerned between two contexts for conflict, including cooperative and competitive. In a competitive context, the objective is winning, with rewards for outcome. In this context, opponents may misperceive intentions leading to suspicion and guardedness. This promotes the antithesis of what constructive differencing can serve but requires those involved to remain open and curious.

In a cooperative context, conflicts are often resolved constructively, because participants are working toward a resolution with mutual goals. The objective of maintaining good working relationships is as important as the outcome.

The difference between these two contexts is often what determines the path of the conflict. Thus our attention is returned to the school culture, including the climate of a particular classroom and the overall milieu of the school itself. It should be evident by now that students will not likely learn to manage conflicts constructively when their school experience is competitive and individualistic.

A tool that can help promote greater cooperative conflict while bringing fun and cohesion to a school may be part of the answer. The future of cooperative conflict resolution is www.ufeud.com. With a name that sparks images of intense dispute but content that may attract the most philosophical of graduate students, Ufeud has something for everybody interested in exploring differences.

For a culture based on democratic principles, we rely on our citizens to challenge establishment, providing public checks and balances for our legislators. We must teach our students how to question the status quo and learn to think critically so they can take over when it's their time. There are many challenging issues facing our country such as cloning, genetically modified organisms, and the use of technology, that may not be resolved in our lifetime. We need this next generation to know how to look at the long-term implications of decisions that benefit those who are like and unlike themselves.

Countries go to war because they cannot work through philosophical, religious, and political differences. If we have any hope of averting a global catastrophe, we need strategic thinkers who can appreciate other perspectives and strategize creative solutions to issues. To create strategic thinkers, we need to begin the training process for appreciating and reconciling differences very early in their school careers.

If academic controversies are bred in schools as part of students' daily learning, students will come to treat differences as instructive as opposed to threatening. Without using conflict as part of the learning environment, it's unlikely that optimal cognitive, social, and moral development can occur. "Academic *controversy* exists when one student's ideas, information, conclusions, theories, and opinions are incompatible with those of another, and the two seek to reach an agreement."[5]

We also want to teach our young people how to deal with more immediate interpersonal differences in a constructive way, without resorting to aggression. If young people can approach differences with curiosity as opposed to threats, they may walk away learning how to overtly influence others and feel more powerful. The result of feeling powerful is not resorting to dramatic demonstrations of their potency.

Young people have difficulty with:

- Expanding their perspective beyond themselves
- Not feeling threatened by differences
- Critically thinking about different positions
- Discerning what is credible, data-driven evidence
- Discriminating between an instinct and a belief
- Feeling confident in a position they aren't in the majority with and
- Considering long-term implications of decisions.

UFeud is a site designed specifically for academic institutions. UFeud promotes creative and interactive self-expression, with the opportunity for measured feedback. Students will learn debating skills that will prepare them with the critical-thinking skills needed to succeed in the world. Some of the goals for the site aimed at helping students include:

- Assimilating the perspective of others
- Thinking through a position and advocating for it
- Creating powerful, well-thought-out arguments
- Developing a unique belief and value system
- Understanding oneself better
- Engaging with others who share similar and opposing perspectives
- Resolving conflicts peaceably and proactively

- Learning how to appreciate and build relationships with those unlike them
- Improving negotiations skills
- Channeling energy away from mindless social media to something more constructive
- Exposing students to world issues
- Giving kids a voice in local and global matters
- Learning to respect those with different opinions
- Learning from other students from across the globe
- Understanding the way statistics are used in business and politics, and
- Pioneering social change.

What separates Ufeud from other sites is its ability to acquire specific results about issues, opinions, beliefs, or other forms of self-expression from people around the globe. UFeud takes social networking to the next level by offering formulated analysis of social-interaction styles to be used for improving the potency of one's argument, enhancing the impact of negotiation, and elevating the level of meaningful debate.

UFeud members can influence public opinion, resolve differences, find others who share similar and contrasting perspectives, and promote ideas to the world. Members can post videos or text-based messages, vote on topics, and create virtual communities called FeudGroups. These are public or private groups on specific topics of interest for a focused gathering of individuals.

UFeud brings together world news with personal opinion. In an era of online social interaction, young people want to be a part of the story and not just read about it. UFeud members can debate sports in real time as the game is being played, join the political debates of our national leaders, and influence the way television and movies are being enjoyed. With a growing need for immediacy and sustained attention, Ufeud offers real time streaming of data.

Imagine a classroom full of social studies students watching and debating right alongside a presidential debate or a group of students in a music appreciation class whose assignment is to watch a video and then debate the difference between Beethoven and Eminem.

FeudGroups are public or private groups on Ufeud devoted to specific topics, or clusters of people for focused debating. A FeudGroup can cover an event such as a presidential race, or it can be an established group like a school's senior social studies class. FeudGroups can be ongoing or a onetime event, such as the high school musical. FeudGroups can also be named in ways that are easy to remember (i.e., www.UFeud.com/Education). There are two types of FeudGroups—public and private.

Undoubtedly the most instrumental aspect of this site in the prevention of youth violence is the Feuder Profile. Automatic generation of feedback helps the user realize personality characteristics and how they are likely to relate with others of similar and different typologies. The Feuder Profile is the first of its kind on the Internet and unique to social networking. Now young people can engage in provocative discussions with others from any part of the planet and learn about themselves at the same time.

As young people can better appreciate how they are being perceived by others, how their style of dealing with differences helps and hinders relationship formation, and how to improve their negotiation and problem-solving skills, they will become more constructive conflict navigators.

With adolescents who don't immediately look for support from others who think like them, demonizing those who think differently, doors open for deeper appreciation of differences. Teens will no longer be threatened by those who disagree with them, and new perspectives will broaden their own way of seeing the world. Critical-thinking skills will be expedited because they will have more information outside their purview to consider.

All this gain will be accomplished while teens are simply enjoying a medium they are highly familiar with. Lesson plans can easily be built around this tool; it can serve as a practice ground for public speaking and will also aid in research skills.

For schools more sensitive to privacy concerns, Ufeud is designed for portability and high level security. Uframes are advanced technology bringing the unique debate platform to any blog, forum, or website on the Internet, in a matter of minutes. Teachers can embed these custom debate templates onto the school website or a custom site of their own to promote private and manageable engagement on any topic the educator selects or creates.

A chief proponent of using debate to improve education and better prepare our children is the current Secretary of Education, Arne Duncan. During a 2012 dinner with the National Association with Urban Debate Leagues he said the following:

> In a number of respects, competitive urban debate is almost uniquely suited to building what's been called the "Four C's" of twenty-first-century skills—critical thinking, communication, collaboration, and creativity. And to that list I might add a fifth "C"—for civic awareness and engagement.
>
> As everyone here knows, preparation for debate not only involves intensive research but advanced critical thinking. Because debate is a contest of ideas—and because students have to switch sides during the debate from arguing against a proposition to defending it—debate forces students to anticipate their opponents' strongest arguments and rebut them with evidence.

That forces students to think deeply about both sides of an issue—and it teaches them to be good listeners. You can't refute an argument if you don't understand it. And I have to add, if more folks in Congress displayed these skills and discipline, our country would be better served.

At the same time, developing an argument pushes student debaters to set a goal and a series of intermediate steps to reach it. Like great leaders, great debaters—to paraphrase the Confucian metaphor—know how to move a mountain one spoonful at a time.

To succeed in debate, you also have to be a creative thinker. You have to spot the gaps that other people don't see—and then fill in those gaps.

Finally, you have to communicate your position clearly and persuasively to judges from different backgrounds and perspectives—whether they are teachers, parents, community leaders, or college students.

And you have to communicate in a collaborative manner. You work with your team.

Arne Duncan is also quoted as saying, "There is no reason to expect, however, that the process will be easy or quick. It took thirty years to reduce smoking in America. It took twenty years to reduce drunk driving. It may take even longer to ensure that children and adolescents can manage conflicts constructively. The more years that students spend learning and practicing the skills of peer mediation and conflict resolution, the more likely they will be to actually use those skills both in the classroom and beyond the school door."[6]

QUESTIONS TO CONSIDER

1. How often do teachers use real-life examples from social media to exemplify what bullying is and how destructive it can be?
2. How much effort has the school put into educating parents around the use of social media, and how it can be an equally destructive tool as it is a constructive one?
3. Has the school even used social media to generate learning around constructive differencing, negotiation, and constructive conflict resolution?
4. How might the school use tools such as Ufeud to promote social learning as well as other valuable academic skills such as supporting arguments with evidence and clear articulation of ideas?

NOTES

1. Posted by "Seneca" UFeud, www.UFeud.com/Seneca.
2. Rabbi Schuly Yanklowitz, "Developing Cognitive Competence: Learning the Skills of Argument," *Huffington Post*, August 15, 2013, http://www.

huffingtonpost.com/rabbi-shmuly-yanklowitz/.

3. M. Deutsch, *The Resolution of Conflict* (New Haven, CT: Yale University Press, 1973).

4. D. W. Johnson and R. Johnson, *Cooperation and Competition: Theory and Research* (Edina, MN: Interaction Book Company, 1989).

5. D. W. Johnson and R. Johnson, *Creative Controversy: Intellectual Challenge in the Classroom* (Edina, MN: Interaction Book Company, 1992).

6. ED.gov, The Power of Debate building the Five "C's" for the 21st Century, April 12, 2012, http://www.ed.gov/news/speeches/power-debatebuilding-five-cs-21st-century.

FIFTEEN
Early-Warning Violence Detection and Prevention

Before another program, punishment, or expensive piece of equipment is purchased, it's time to consider a more expansive model of prevention. Through our reverse-profiling lens, we make a case for how to conceptualize the processes that influence the potential for violence. We make connections with the contextual factors including school culture, community, family, and societal influences in how they collide with intra- and interpersonal dynamics, sparking the perfect storm. And because many of the larger contextual influences such as the media and entertainment are unlikely to change significantly any time soon, we can predict that a strong foundation is being developed for even more catastrophic violence to form.

Since we cannot rely on lawmakers to improve legislation in the short term that will make it easier for schools to be safer, we must figure out how to do this for ourselves. In spite of driving forces for standardization, such as the common core curriculum, we continue paddling up river, fighting a very heavy opposing current. Putting so much energy into compliance, adapting our work to fit the parameters set forth by those who feel well out of touch with the classroom, leaves educators feeling drained, powerless, and without much hope. Due to this surging pressure that burns teachers out well before their prime and discourages others who might consider entering the profession, we cannot burden them with more work. Any system being implemented must fit their existing infrastructure and not cause more feelings of frustration.

Yet we must also shift our focus to ensure measuring the right information and all the data available to us, which by this point may seem voluminous. If schools can shift their focus from trying to identify the next potential shooter to appreciating the risk factors inherent in the school, we will create a paradigm shift that moves us much closer to a reliable early-warning prevention model. This is going to require a change in ideology, more so than any logistical work, which can be time consuming and tedious.

So rather than training faculty in the latest program that may or may not have validity, may or may not address the specific types of violence seen in the school, or may or may not help improve the culture and bolster the students to feel safer and resilient, it's time to create an actual learning community—not simply for the students, but for the adults who also need to be learning parallel to the children. The adults need to be learning about the specific needs of their students, how to reach kids in distress, how to negotiate with administers to have a stronger voice in the direction of the school, and how to understand when a student is seriously at risk.

All this can be done with a minimal amount of work if the ideas produce buy-in. If the ideas in this book have stirred your interest, you can use that momentum to stimulate the curiosity of others who are also likely looking for hope. There will always be resistance to change and that's healthy; otherwise we would be in constant chaos without any sense of grounding. Patience then is a helpful part of this movement that will inspire others to open their eyes to new possibility, reminding them of why they entered this profession to start with.

An early-warning detection and prevention system for violence is more than just a way to make schools safer; it's a way to make them healthier. The best way to prevent colds is to eat right, get enough rest, engage in regular exercise, and reduce stress. The most effective way to reduce school violence is to nourish and support the system, provide effective teaching for students on how to navigate differences, and improve resiliency so that threats are dealt with constructively and not impulsively. Through the generation of cooperative conflict resolution, identification of risk factors, continuous scanning of one's environment, and putting into action the lessons being learned on a daily basis, each school can become a stronger institution that children and adults want to protect.

Another vital component for an effective early-warning system is the inclusion of data from students and parents. It has been well established that past perpetrators have indicated to somebody through some method their plans to cause serious damage. Whether it was through a journal, online message, social-networking post, or seemingly casual comment made by phone or in person, young people intent on serious disruption want others to know about it. These potential perpetrators wanted others to know and watch for what was coming.

Even more so, these students didn't wake up one day and decide to exact revenge on the school. Quite the contrary, these events have been well planned and orchestrated through weeks and months of preparation. During this time, and most importantly the time preceding their decision to kill, these students had grievances that were not being addressed. Whether their unhappiness stemmed from events at home, at school, with peers, or with teachers, they were losing hope that anybody cared and that anything could be done.

An effective early-warning system needs to include an active hotline for students and families to be able to notify somebody of an impending threat. This system also needs to offer support for those students who are in distress but not yet at the point of doing anything harmful to themselves or others. No matter how healthy the school culture is, adolescence is a tumultuous time of identity formation and social acceptance, leaving children at risk for a multitude of mental health concerns. In particular for those students who don't have strong family support, resources need to be made available to help students during critical times in their lives, even if it's to simply link them with services.

Communication with and among all the students, parents, and faculty is currently done through portals and email. This system seems efficient for parents who don't have matching times to contact teachers and allows educators to respond into the evening if they so choose. The stigma of this form of communication is formal, discouraging those who are in distress or fear being identified.

There are phone lines available for students who want to report a concern or are in crisis, but not all students are aware of them. Nor is the information able to be fully utilized by the school because it remains private at whatever call center in the country fields it.

If students felt comfortable conveying information about their experience of the school culture, such as their peer groups, teachers, and administrators, there could be an entirely useful data stream ready to consider. Students are the consumers of services in an educational institution, and, like any organization that has customers, it would do well to consider feedback. This may be an unappealing idea for administrators who don't want to encourage complaining; however, if students were taught to vocalize or deliver their messages in a constructive way that includes feelings and suggestions, it can be another good learning opportunity.

If enough students and families were to be delivering the same messages, themes might emerge that could help school officials better understand chronic issues needing attention. Students and parents ought to be able to designate who the message is sent to but learn how to address the source first before going up the ladder.

QUESTIONS TO CONSIDER

1. What current methods does the school have for detecting violence potential?

2. Do you consider your school a learning *organization* or simply a community that promotes teaching? Organizations require attention to systems and processes, which you want to consider how well you attend to.
3. How much information have you gained from those outside the school to improve your awareness about the culture within? How would you use this information if you knew how to solicit it?
4. If catastrophic violence were to take place in your school, what would you look back and wish you would have addressed?

SIXTEEN
Potential-for-Violence Inventory (PVI)

DATA COLLECTION

The first step in creating an early-warning violence-detection and prevention system is identifying the school's protective and risk factors. Similar to what we do with a particular youth or subset of young people, we too want to first assess the contextual variables around school culture. In measuring the various planes of influence, we will utilize our reverse-profiling methodology, starting with a big picture, working our way down to a more precise figure.

Schools currently track basic student information such as grades, tardiness, discipline, and other highly observable and recordable information. They are not, however, tracking (in a measurable format) the quality of a student's work, the degree of aggression embodied in a student's writing, the changes in socialization, the significant changes in family dynamics, the student's level of emotional detachment, and many other factors that could be of value in detecting downward spirals.

Schools are not currently equipped to gather the type of data needed to effectively utilize the reverse-profiling method. Unlike traditional profiling, which can be done by one person who is building upward from minute data, reverse profiling is starting with a broader picture to make more refined deductions. This requires multiple information streams measuring diverse data points and examining variables schools rarely look at, such as community–school relations, societal influences, family-of-origin issues, matters pertaining to school culture, and the impact of other significant extrinsic influences.

Data from teacher perceptions of the school culture are also not gathered, leaving out this very important contextual component that can influence a student toward or away from violence. Schools don't have any quantifiable way of measuring school culture aside from surveys that are sometimes done by administrators but lacking the objectivity and scope needed for a valid picture to be created.

Schools are not yet using this reverse-profiling method, because their current data-collection methods and existing databases look for information around static variables as opposed to fluid trends and patterns. For instance, a school is tracking a student's grades each marking period, but it isn't tracking the elevation of violent writing or increase in social isolation. Schools aren't inputting information that is crucial to finding impending deterioration because they are operating under a one-dimensional data-collection system that only reveals a partial picture of student health.

Schools are not measuring the intersection of variables because they are tracking data that is flat. When you compile data that is purely demographic and conceptually unrelated, the data becomes one-dimensional. For instance, a school likely keeps records on absenteeism but does not input the qualitative measurement of missing school as it relates to a recent traumatic event in the student's life. Before we collect data, we want to know what the data will be used for. Trying to make sense out of existing statistics can work, but missing information is almost always a barrier to having a fuller picture.

School personnel are not interested in new systems that are burdensome and time consuming, which means the inputting of data needs to be quick and simple. The work to install an early-warning detection system comprised of all the elements outlined in this book is remarkably easy and not nearly as time intensive as most prevention programs available today. The key is in how we collect and use the data, recognizing that there will be some variation for schools that have unique attributes.

There are benefits to creating a uniform system of data collection; however, the uniqueness of each school makes that challenging. Rather than restricting the school to taking the same measurements, it may be more helpful to outline the areas in which information needs to be collected so that the school can design its own system that works for it. Because of student privacy needs, there is certain information that would be useful but is unattainable. Information such as the prescription of medications, the diagnosis of mental illness, the reports from outside resources such as community mental health services, and other psychological information is also restricted in how it is used.

An outline of the dimension being measured and the sample questions to elicit this information is listed below. The dimensions and factors ought to look familiar by this point because they have each been addressed in great detail. It's important to note that any school-wide survey would not be completed all at once but gradually over time, allowing for continuous examination and reflection. We also want to remain aware that answers may change over time due to varying perspectives, so we want a continuous stream of data as opposed to a snapshot at any particular point in time.

Comparing answers from administrators, teachers, and other faculty members can yield more useful data. People in different positions will likely have varied perspectives, letting school leaders know that congruence and harmony are less likely.

While school-climate-assessment surveys can be used to gather similar data, many of these inventories are incomplete, measuring only certain aspects of school culture such as the climate. Use the questions below as a guide for getting beyond paper-and-pen assessments, which oftentimes lose value due to resistance on the par of faculty. Teachers wonder if their hard work in filling out a survey will actually result in any changes being made and therefore put less effort into formulating their answers.

Having conversations with staff members around these topics can demonstrate that leadership is serious about applying learning from the captured data. Finding creative ways to gather and assimilate the abundance of information about school culture alone will be a sizeable task, one that requires a strong commitment on the part of leadership.

Adaptation	**Climate**	**Infrastructure**	**Miscellaneous**
Professional Development	Morale	Leadership	Faculty
Team/Decision Making	Job Satisfaction	Supervision	Students
Resiliency	Philosophical Accord	Policy/Procedure	
Structure	Communication	Physical Environment	
Learning	Autonomy/ Empowerment	Integrity/Values	

POTENTIAL-FOR-VIOLENCE INVENTORY (PVI)

Dimension I: School Culture

Adaptation

  A. Professional Development

- Educators are generally satisfied with school-sponsored training and Professional Development (PD).
- Educators are satisfied with school-sponsored training around issues pertaining to violence prevention.
- Educators are satisfied with school mental health professionals' assistance in identifying and helping at-risk students.

- The school offers effective training for faculty regarding diversity.
- Faculty and students are generally aware of the guidelines to confidentiality when speaking with school personnel about serious emotional and behavior issues.
- There has been a recent or gradual worsening in professional-development opportunities.

B. Team Efficacy/Decision Making

- Faculty meetings are conducted regularly with the entire faculty and seem productive.
- Faculty meetings are well organized and efficient but flexible to deal with immediate issues.
- Faculty meetings offer safe opportunities to discuss differing perspectives, feel safe to differ with others, and seem to build cohesion among the staff.
- Conflicts often find satisfactory resolution during staff meetings.
- Faculty address the problems directly and without subgrouping or carrying grudges.
- The faculty is mostly cohesive and does not engage in territorial or clique-oriented disputes.
- Personality differences are addressed openly and with little hostility.
- There has been a recent or gradual erosion of the faculty decision-making processes

C. Resiliency

- If the school were to experience a traumatic event, the school would likely recover quickly and fully.
- The school seems to respond well to change and adversity.
- The school has experienced significant challenges in recent months.
- The students on the whole seem to bounce back well from disappointment.
- The school seems less likely to recover quickly from a trauma than it would have weeks or months ago.

D. Structure

- Faculty members generally know what is expected of them and have clear guidelines on how to handle most situations.
- There is an adequate level of support but not so much oversight that the school feels rigid.
- The school does a good job of keeping transitions smooth as opposed to thrusting major changes with little preparation.

- The school seems to be less flexible than it did in the past.

E. Learning

- The faculty and administration learn from their mistakes.
- There is an active process of examining new policies and practices to evaluate their efficacy.
- Faculty are open to the feedback from the students.
- Administrators seem receptive and interested in feedback from faculty.
- There seems to be less interest in learning on the part of the faculty than in the recent past.
- The school seems to make the same mistakes over and over again.

Climate

A. Morale

- The faculty feels cohesive in its working relationships.
- People seem to enjoy coming to work each day.
- There is a good working relationship between faculty and administration.
- Students seem to feel a part of the school community.
- The vibe when you walk through the hallways is generally positive.
- There has been a recent or fairly recent change in staff morale.

B. Job Satisfaction

- I like most aspects of my job and my place of employment.
- There are more aspects of my job that I like than dislike.
- Faculty members seem to go above and beyond with their work because they feel invested.
- The workload is manageable on most days.
- There is sufficient variety and opportunity for growth in my job.
- I have felt worse about my job over recent weeks and months.
- I like my job less this year than I have in years past.

C. Philosophical Accord

- I know what the mission and vision of my school are, and they are spoken about during the school year.
- The mission and vision of the school are reflected in the policies and procedures.

- As a staff we generally believe in the work we are doing and feel like the district has an agenda that supports our efforts.
- There seems to be a widening gap between what I feel my values are with the school's practices.

D. *Communication*

- There is bidirectional feedback between faculty and administration.
- There is bidirectional feedback between faculty and students.
- The administration encourages and is receptive to suggestions and concerns from faculty.
- The administration is clear, direct, and honest with faculty.
- There has been a recent or gradual decline in the communication between faculty and administration.
- There has been a recent or gradual decline in the communication between faculty and students.

E. *Autonomy/Empowerment*

- Teachers feel they have a reasonable amount of independence to be creative and innovative in their work.
- Teachers feel supported by administrators to contribute to the school beyond their classrooms.
- Administrators feel supported by the district with a reasonable amount of freedom to run their schools.
- There has been a recent or gradual decline in teacher autonomy.

Infrastructure

A. *Leadership*

- The school has strong leadership in the principal and superintendent.
- The faculty and students seem to respect the administrators.
- The school is well connected to the community and is utilizing all its community resources.
- The school has a better reputation because of its leaders.
- Leadership does a good job in building a cohesive team.
- Leadership does a good job in shaping a healthy school culture.
- Leadership is personable, honest, and well meaning.
- The school doesn't feel as well run as it once did.
- There is constant turnover for school administrators.

B. *Supervision*
- Faculty receive supervision when needed and believe it is helpful.
- Faculty utilize their supervisors for professional development.
- Faculty members find their evaluations useful to their professional growth.
- Faculty members consider the feedback they receive through evaluations to be fair and objective.
- The quality and consistency of supervision has declined in the recent past.

C. *Policies and Procedures*
- Parents have a clear process for communicating with teachers and voicing complaints.
- Students have a clear and well-established process for voicing complaints.
- Parents and students are made aware of potential policy changes prior to implementation.
- Students and parents are provided with written guidelines for school policies and procedures.
- Faculty are familiar with policies and procedures, which overall seem to make for smoother operations.
- The policy and procedure manual is reviewed regularly and updated with the input of faculty and parents.
- The school has a clear policy for bullying that is considered effective by faculty.
- Policies and procedures seem outdated and have not been well enforced recently.

D. *Physical Environment*
- The school building is clean and neat the majority of the time.
- The school feels warm and inviting.
- The school has enough physical security features to help it feel safe.
- The school has reasonably close access for law enforcement to arrive quickly in emergencies.
- The school seems to have deteriorated physically over recent months.

E. *Integrity/Values*
- The school represents itself to the public in a way that reflects its true values and operations.

- Administrators and faculty are respectful to students and encourage open exploration of differences.
- Differences are recognized and celebrated among the staff and students.
- The school seems to do what it purports to do the majority of the time.
- The school seems to have degraded with regard to integrity and values.

Miscellaneous

- An Employee Assistance Program (EAP) or other vehicle for finding personal resources in the community is available to faculty.
- The school offers curriculum for students regarding issues of diversity.
- Parents are generally viewed as supports for student education as opposed to hindrances. Good working relationships exist with most parents.
- A mentoring and/or tutoring system is in place by peers and by faculty.
- Faculty is provided with a directory of services it provides to parents of at-risk youth.
- Community providers offer informational seminars to school personnel to increase awareness of existing resources.
- Sufficient community resources exist to involve youth in after-school activities and support for dealing with problems.
- Surveys of the student body are taken on a regular basis to assist in assessing student needs.
- Surveys of parents are conducted regularly to assess satisfaction with services.
- Surveys of teachers are conducted regularly to assess organizational effectiveness.
- The school uses a peer-mediation program, which is viewed as useful by the staff, parents, and faculty.
- Students with academic problems are quickly recognized and dealt with in an efficient and sensitive manner.

Miscellaneous for Students

- The student body has a forum to voice their concerns about daily operations.
- Students are regularly recognized for both achievement and improvement.

- Students have an anonymous place to voice concerns about issues, including other students.
- Students have a way of communicating with teachers outside of class time.
- Students are helped to work through differences with other students through coaching and mediation by faculty.

Dimension II: Student Data

Academic

A. Absenteeism

- Student has recent erratic school attendance.
- Student has missed days when he/she usually is consistently present.
- Student has missed school but not brought absent note.
- Student has odd or no reasons for missing school.
- Student had extended absence.

B. Tardiness

- Student has recent erratic tardiness.
- Student has been late when he/she usually is consistently present.
- Student has been late but not brought absent note.
- Student has odd or no reasons for being late.
- Student had extended streak of tardiness.

C. Turning in Work

- Student has recent erratic work completion.
- Student has been late in turning in assignments when typically on time.
- Student's work quality has recently deteriorated.
- Student has recently turned in work that has themes of violence.

Academic	**Relationships**	**Behavior**	**Miscellaneous**
Absenteeism	Isolation	Discipline	Family
Tardiness	Bullying	Disrespect	Trauma/Loss
Turning in Work	Bullied	Withdrawn	Ufeud
Declining Grades	Fights	Peculiar	Mental Health
Cheating	Peer Group	Detached	Medication

- Student has recently turned in work that is odd or peculiar.

D. Declining Grades

- Student has had a recent decline in test scores or graded papers.
- Student seems to care less about the grades he/she receives.
- Student seems less interested in revising work for better grades.
- Student seems concerned about reaction from family about grades.

E. Cheating

- Student has recently been noticed to be cheating on tests.
- Student has recently been attempting to cheat on assignments.
- Student has recently allowed others to copy off his/her tests.
- Student has recently allowed others to copy off his/her assignments.

Relationships

A. Isolation

- Student has recently become disinterested in socializing.
- Student has had peers express concern about him/her.

B. Bullying

- Student has recently been picking on others.
- Student is becoming feared by his/her peers.

C. Bullied

- Student has recently become a target of others to pick on.
- Student is seemingly responding differently to teasing.

D. Fights

- Student has recently been involved with physical altercations.
- Student has recently been involved with verbal jousting with others.

E. Peer Group

- Student has recently made a change in peer group.
- Student only has one person he/she associates with.

- Student seems antagonistic toward other peers groups.

Behavior

A. Discipline

- Student has been in trouble more often recently.
- Student has suddenly stopped being a discipline problem.

B. Disrespect

- Student seems to care less about respecting authority.
- Student has recently been uncharacteristically rude to adults.

C. Withdrawn

- Student has pulled away from adults he/she was once close to.
- Student has pulled away from peers he/she was once close to.

D. Peculiar

- Student has been acting strangely of late.
- Student seems different in a way that's hard to describe.

E. Detached

- Student seems disaffected by academic stimuli.
- Student seems emotionally numb in recent weeks.

Miscellaneous

A. Family

- Student has reported recent changes to his/her family such as addiction.
- Student has recently reported feeling distant from family.

B. Trauma/Loss

- Student has recently lost a close friend or family member.
- Student is dealing with parents' separation or divorce.

C. History of Depression

- Student has made it known that he/she has thought about harming him/herself.

- Student has admitted to cutting or other self-injurious behavior.

D. *Mood Medication*
- Student has been on medication for depression in the past.
- Student has recently been put on medication for depression.

DATA ASSIMILATION

Once all the pertinent data is collected or is in the process of being collected, there is the crucial question about how to interpret this information. From the numerous areas being considered, it may be evident that no single person will be able to synthesize the data in a way that helps make meaning of it. There are too many variables, creating complex constellations that are too highly subjective to make even general inferences for the untrained analyst.

The software needs to be simple to employ, require very little time on the part of the inputters (educators), and be processed through algorithms that identify key downward trends of concern. The data needs to be seen as evolutionary, meaning that we don't want to look at any moment in time in isolation but instead see it as a process that is moving a school closer or further from organizational health.

Educators are always weary about being asked to do more with less time. They are also going to be fearful of retaliation should they evaluate their school or leader in a less favorable light. Because of this, data needs to have protections of anonymity, with regard to the first dimension of school culture. Otherwise faculty won't feel comfortable being truthful. There also needs to be summative information provided back to faculty members so they see how their perspective compares with that of others. Too often, surveys such as job satisfaction are conducted within organizations that don't yield any observable results, making them feel like exercises in futility. If the teachers better understand what is being done with the results, the administrators will be held accountable but they won't be solely responsible—meaning that it's the job of the entire faculty to improve school culture and the administrator is going to serve as the facilitator of dialogue around the growth process.

Reverse profiling means looking at the big picture and drilling down to make connections with specific occurrences. The big picture involves a mid-level exploration of school culture as it relates to organizational health so we can better appreciate the context in which troubled students are being either nurtured to health or marginalized to promote acting out. School culture is complex in itself to measure, and once we add the dimension of time, we are now faced with understanding the cycles and patterns that improve and detract from a healthy and stable school culture.

Educators and administrators are not able to see subtle shifts in school culture because they are living it every day. When we are inside of a process, we tend to become less attuned to the gradual trends taking place, especially when we are so focused on content. Schools are content and outcome focused, making them less inclined to see and understand process, in particular from a child's perspective. And because of the multiple subcultures that get created in each classroom, it can be very challenging to attend to the amalgamation of all those microcosms into a larger constellation. A child can experience one classroom as warm and nurturing but another classroom as hostile and threatening. This doesn't mean that the classroom is that way; it means, based on his specific set of parameters, the child perceives it that way.

Schools need mechanisms to understand both their subcultures and larger cultures so they can appreciate how children behave. If schools want their students to report concerns about a classmate who seems distressed and possibly suicidal or homicidal, they must realize that the school culture will influence whether disclosures will be made.

In the PVI outlined in the data-collection section, there were three dimensions of school culture with five specific factors within each dimension. As faculty members rate these areas along with the specific data in the second dimension around student trends, they are creating a profile of themselves as well as of the school/student. Each time a question is answered about the school or student, a perspective is being created that's both a reflection of outward and inward data.

How we view something tells us a lot about ourselves. If I hold up a baseball, for instance, and one person sees it nostalgically, with warm memories of playing ball with their father in the backyard, but another person sees it as a reminder of being tormented on the schoolyard because he wasn't athletically inclined, we are getting two different pictures of the same image. It's still a baseball, but what it means to each person is to be shaped by their own life experiences that therefore influence how they perceive that item.

Now consider a nontangible item that isn't nearly as simple as a baseball. Imagine all the complex circuitry that makes up school culture and our individual perspectives of this ambiguous entity. Imagine that most schools may feel threatened by this idea because it means looking at the school in a way that may feel threatening or blaming. Add in the variability of how people experience an entity or event, creating such diversity that agreement on what is actual may not be a realistic goal. Because of these influences, we ought not use this tool as a concrete evaluation that ranks schools or categorizes them in red ink. Instead, we are looking for dialogue based on heightened awareness that can lead to meaningful exchanges rather than increased hostility and fragmentation.

This is an important point for readers who work in schools, accustomed to standardized testing and reporting. In an era in which schools are rated continuously with the intent of holding them more accountable, we may have gone to the far end of the continuum for data assimilation. All data and results interpretations need to be viewed as pieces of information as opposed to concrete representations of an entire picture. Data can be misleading if we aren't well versed in how to use it.

If the majority of people favorably evaluate an aspect of school culture the same way, we can make inferences about the overall picture of that school. Leadership, for instance, may be rated as 90 percent favorable by faculty within a school, leading one to determine that the administrators are doing a fine job of being fair and objective. If we look closely at the 10 percent who rated the administrator unfavorably, adding in the variables of a Caucasian principal with the information that the 10 percent were all minorities, we come up with a vastly different hypothetical picture.

This is one simple but powerful example of why the assimilation of data is so crucial to using this tool effectively. We never want to rule in or out hypotheses based on majority perspective when there is so much rich information available on a granular level. Each teacher that rates a child or school culture is in effect rating herself. Our perspective on something is a synthesis of the raw data seen through a unique filter made up of our experiences, values, beliefs, character, and other variables. Looking at how we see somebody or something is always a reflection of who we are if we are willing to look and know what to look for.

Take a teacher, for instance, who is in that 10 percent minority rating the school administrator unfavorably. If that teacher also sees a summary of his data input around school culture and students as significantly lower than his colleagues, he may want to consider what is helping him to be more critical or discerning. Perhaps the students feel like they can't please this teacher or it's too hard to live up to what they consider to be unrealistic expectations. Or perhaps the administrator rarely provides constructive feedback because she is afraid the teacher will take it as threatening (because this is the vibe she gives off herself). A tool that provides feedback to the person inputting the data makes it more dynamic and useful.

PRIVACY CONCERNS

Whenever we collect, store, and interpret data on school students we must be mindful of privacy and civil rights. If we collect data that may be useful for identifying downward trends for students, we are going to raise questions about compliance with the Family Education Rights and Privacy Act (FERPA). This becomes especially important when considering what information is shared between schools and with parents, and what becomes a part of the student's permanent record.

Ongoing dialogue will be needed as privacy and safety concerns seesaw with every new catastrophic event. Just as the Department of Homeland Security has infringed on certain rights of privacy, such as monitoring phone calls for US citizens and world leaders abroad, all in the interest of national security, so too will we have this issue contested in our schools.

While we enter this new phase of violence prevention as it intersects with privacy, we need to stay mindful that information is used and not misused. This means those who have access to the information need to be trained, that information is protected so that hackers can't infiltrate the software, and that there need to be established guidelines about what the information is used for. The idea is not to cause alarm but to send up red flags.

The focus first and foremost needs to be on the school system as opposed to having a screening tool that helps officials disregard the underlying causes of student violence. As we have learned through our study of school violence, there is going to be less chance of identifying the next school shooter because standard profiles for these perpetrators do not exist. There is, however, a greater likelihood of identifying a school in which conditions are right for violence to take place. Just as we issue a tornado watch when conditions are right for the formation of a twister, so too can we create a reverse-profiling prevention model that helps us understand what schools are at risk, the specific risk factors, and what can be done to help grow the school toward greater organizational health.

IMPLEMENTATION: REVERSE PROFILING

Here are some concrete recommendations on how to implement a reverse profiling approach in your school.

A. Society Level

- Create lessons on the constructive and destructive uses of social media. Parents need to be part of these classes and sign off on supervising their students.
- As part of the class, have students brainstorm on how to make social media safer for students to prevent the use of this medium for harassment. Have the students send letters to the social networking sites to practice their letter writing and advocacy skills.

B. School Level

- Students need a safe place to reach out when they are worried about another student, and lessons need to be done on reporting concerns of behavior or suicidal intent.
- Ensure that violence-prevention programs are prescreened for research-based efficacy, and implement these programs with care.
- Ensure that violence-prevention programs match the type of violence most likely seen in the school.
- Consider whether the mission/vision statement for school includes attention to school culture.
- Include in regular faculty meetings dialogue about school culture. Include discussion of processes, patterns, cycles, and other systems-related perspectives.
- Administrators would benefit from training and/or supervision in group dynamics to serve as stronger facilitators for these process meetings.
- Gain input from new faculty members, teachers, and students regarding school culture.
- Ensure that tip lines are well promoted within the school so that students can anonymously warn of impending violence or other threat.
- Improve communication tools between parents and teachers so that a collaborative process can take place for students in distress.

SUMMARY

Whether you are selecting an existing violence-prevention program or designing something tailor made for your school, there are several pillars to build from:

1. Develop a paradigm grounded in theory.
2. Consider the types of violence most prevalent in your school. Consider how to assess for this data if you aren't certain.
3. Make certain to use a reverse-profiling method inclusive of all areas such as school culture, student behavior, community, and family.
4. Involve your entire community, from parents to students, to ensure the program is comprehensive and well invested.
5. Remember the important elements of a violence-prevention paradigm before selecting or developing a program that fits your school.
6. Identify patterns, trends, cycles, and other changes measured over time to identify risk factors. Children don't become killers overnight.

7. Continuously assess your program on every level so your program never becomes static or complacent. Remember to look beyond the school walls to include cyberbullying.
8. Balance physical safety measures with improvements to organizational health.
9. Don't be afraid to use outside consultants who can lend an objective perspective while introducing unbiased suggestions.
10. Develop a school philosophy that incorporates models of nonviolence, upstander values, and an anonymous warning system for potential threats.

www.ingramcontent.com/pod-product-compliance
Lightning Source LLC
Chambersburg PA
CBHW021801230426
43669CB00006B/155